EVERYONE
WELCOME*

*CERTAIN RESTRICTIONS APPLY

ROGER   HERNANDEZ

Pacific Press®
Publishing Association

Nampa, Idaho | Oshawa, Ontario, Canada
www.pacificpress.com

Cover design by Gerald Lee Monks
Cover design resources from iStockphoto.com
Interior design by Aaron Troia

The author assumes full responsibility for the accuracy of all facts and quotations as cited in this book.

You can obtain additional copies of this book by calling toll-free 1-800-765-6955 or by visiting http://www.adventistbookcenter.com.

Library of Congress Cataloging-in-Publication Data
Names: Hernandez, Roger, 1967- author.
Title: Everyone welcome : rediscovering the passion to reach the ones God misses the most / Roger Hernandez.
Description: Nampa : Pacific Press Publishing, 2016.
Identifiers: LCCN 2015045661 | ISBN 9780816361106 (pbk.)
Subjects: LCSH: Generation Y—Religious life. | Church attendance.
Classification: LCC BV4529.2 .H47 2016 | DDC 259/.25—dc23 LC record available at http://lccn.loc.gov/2015045661

January 2016

Contents

Start-up

Every Christian should ask two questions every day:

What breaks my heart?
What am I going to do about it?

This is what breaks my heart. Thirty-eight million Americans have stopped going to church in the past twenty years. Millennials are the least evangelized generation. People have stopped hating the church because they don't even think about it. Why? Older members, empty pews, infighting, apostasy, and a propensity to hurt first and ask questions later. Those are some of the reasons.

That breaks my heart.

This book is my way of diagnosing the problem and providing viable solutions to our problems. You probably won't agree with everything I write here. That is fine. I hope that you can at least consider and talk about the issues we face.

Every chapter contains some feedback from a real-life, in-the-trenches pastor. These are local church pastors with growing churches. They will reflect from their vantage point on the topic of that chapter. They are diverse and multicultural.

Harold Altamirano: Lead pastor for Life Fellowship, a multicultural Adventist congregation in South Florida (www.life-fellowship.com).

Anthony WagenerSmith: Lead pastor and church planter

of LifeSpring Adventist Church in Tampa, Florida, a diverse congregation (www.lifespringadventist.org).

Kymone Hinds: Lead pastor and church planter of Journey Fellowship, an Adventist church in Memphis, Tennessee, as well as pastor of Overton Park, an established African-American church in the same city (www.comejourney.org).

Richie Halversen: Lead pastor of College Drive Seventh-day Adventist Church in Jackson, Mississippi, and church planter of a new congregation in the same city (www.collegedrivechurch.com).

Rebecca Davis: Associate pastor at Berean Church in Atlanta, Georgia, one of the most recognizable and influential African-American churches in North America (www.atlantaberean.com).

Dave Ketelsen: Lead pastor of Hamilton Community Church in Chattanooga, Tennessee, a congregation that consistently attracts young adults (www.hamiltonchurch.com).

Myron Edmonds: Lead pastor and visionary of Glenville Seventh-day Adventist Church in Cleveland, Ohio, a church that is known for community impact (www.gvillesda.org).

Kendall Turcios: Lead pastor and church planter of Ignite Church of Miami, Florida, a church that is geared to reach postmodern people (www.myignitechurch.org).

The book is divided into three parts:

> Problem—an honest look at what ails us

> Plan—four practical solutions

> Preach—a proven approach to a more intentional evangelistic experience.

As you read it, ask yourself these two questions:

What breaks my heart?
What am I going to do about it?

Hybrid

You may identify with the prodigal son, or maybe with the older brother. Some, like me, have a bit of both in us. We are *hybrids,* so to speak. Before we get into the story of a repentant son and a reluctant older brother, allow me to share my personal story. It will give you some insight later on in the book about the deep passion that burns within me for reaching those whom God misses the most. Here is my hybrid story.

We're leaving!

I was born in Cuba, under a tyrant's rule. Even before I was born, my dad knew that he wanted a better life for us, as did my mom. That's why she insisted on naming me Roger, instead of what my dad wanted to call me—Nabucodonosor (Nabuco for short). She said, "One day we will go to America, and I want my son to have an English-sounding name."

I was just two years old when my dad, a pastor, decided to apply for a visa to leave Cuba. What followed for him was hell on earth. He was assigned to a sugarcane-cutting detail that worked six days a week. Every forty-five days, he would come home and spend a weekend with us. Then he would leave again—back to the sixteen-hour days, the lack of food, the harassment from the guards, mosquitoes, and everything that could be the definition of brutal misery. After two years, we finally received good news. Our visa was approved! But timing was not on our side. My mother was pregnant with

9

my brother Isaac—8.3 months pregnant to be exact. The law required her to first have the baby, then travel. But my father had had enough of the tyrant. He had had enough of the secret police, the lack of possibilities, and the impossibility of freedom. So my mom packed all she could in the one *maleta* (suitcase) that we were allowed to take out of the country, put on the biggest dress she could find, and we headed for the airport. Right before we passed the guard who checked the passports, my pants dropped. She bent over to pick them up, and the guard didn't notice the belly with the 10.5-pound baby inside. We got on the plane. Finally, freedom was ours. Freedom came with a price though. It always does. Freedom, by definition, is not just the absence of tyranny but deliverance from it. Deliverance is never easy, but it's worth it. The price *we* paid for freedom was high.

We paid a high financial price. We were only allowed to take from Cuba one piece of luggage. No property deeds. No savings account balance. None of our hard-earned cash. Nothing valuable was to be taken out of the country. We went ahead and did it because we wanted out. We came to the point where we were willing to leave *anything* behind for the *one thing* that meant *everything:* freedom. We also paid a relational price. All our family, loved ones, friends, and coworkers were left behind. We traveled to Spain, where we could count on one hand the people we knew and still have some fingers left over. The desire to be free is even stronger than the "ties that bind." We elected to be free by ourselves, all alone, rather than to be in bondage with our extended family. We paid a price in stability. We went from Cuba to Spain. To Costa Rica. To Miami. To Aibonito, Puerto Rico. To Las Piedras, Guayama, Cayey, and then Cidra, all of them in Puerto Rico. And finally, back to the United States. Those were some of the places and countries where we lived as pastor's kids. We sort of got used to it. "We're moving" seemed to be my father's favorite phrase. We had the same attitude as Elizabeth Taylor toward her husbands: "We won't be staying long." We found support in each other and made many friends along the way. We paid a price in health for freedom. When I was little, my health suffered because of malnutrition. Since food was in short supply in Cuba, especially when my father was gone, my mother gave me a bottle of water and brown sugar at night, to ease the hunger pains. This concoction calmed my hunger but left me with a mouthful of rotten teeth. My father had it the worst. His health suffered the brunt of concentration camp conditions. Any person who, for two years, is undernourished and overworked endures a physical toll that lasts the rest of their life. But it was a price he was willing to pay. I could not have chosen freedom myself. I didn't have the knowledge, ability, strength, or resources to do it. My father did. Thanks to his sacrifice, we have a better life. Thanks to the selfless love of one, many could call freedom a possibility. He gave me the opportunity to dream.

"Cubiche"

We settled on the beautiful island of Puerto Rico. My dad continued to work as a pastor, and my two brothers and I made sure there was never a dull moment in the house. People in my neighborhood called me *"cubiche,"* a slang word for Cuban. I didn't protest (I was only one against many), but the name reminded me of my past. Why think about what I had left? I'd rather concentrate on my new life. I was free from the communist tyrant, but, believe it or not, another tyrant took its place. Its name is legalism, and it was found in the place where you might least expect it: the church.

Rules, rules, rules

I grew up in church. We went to church at least three times a week, sometimes more. Since my dad was also an evangelist, we had months when I spent most nights setting up the three carousels of projector slides, along with a "dissolver" (Google it!). I also set up the movie projector with two reels to show a movie about the dangers of smoking, called *I'm Sorry Baby,* and another one about the life of Jesus that was pretty cool. In those years I got a lot of church but not enough of Christ. I liked going to church. The thing that I struggled with was all the rules and regulations that did not make sense to a teenage boy. They say that rules without relationship lead to rebellion, and that is exactly what happened to me. I was shown the *what* without the *why.* I received knowledge without power. That has three negative consequences:

1. Knowledge without power is frustrating. You never feel secure, because you never know when you have done enough. Should you pray one hour or two? Maybe an all-nighter would be even better. You work toward victory instead of working from victory. There is never a finish line. It's the race where the dog can never reach the rabbit right in front of it. It's like the song says: "Forever running but losing the race . . ."

One of my most vivid memories of growing up is having a constant feeling of guilt. I knew what was right, yet I couldn't do it. That was very frustrating. It happens to plenty of Christians every day. Think about it for a moment.

- Millions know about the dangers of smoking, yet

plenty choose to smoke anyway.
- Millions know about the benefits of going to school, yet many drop out.
- Millions know about the consequences of premarital sex, yet teenage pregnancy is rampant.

We know what to do. But we don't do it. Why? Because information is good but not good enough.

2. *Knowledge without power is dangerous.* It can make you feel superior and act superior. It can make you think that all you need to do to convert someone is to share information with them. I had no problem reciting the eschatological timeline. I could produce all the texts that proved why we were the correct church and Catholics were not. This is dangerous, not because prophetic information is not good (it is), but because, when conversion has not happened, you can use knowledge as a billy club, even if in your own private life you are struggling with secret sin. Ellen White summarizes what happens in an unconverted heart: "There need to be far more lessons in the ministry of the Word of true conversion than of the arguments of the doctrines. For it is far easier and more natural for the heart that is not under the control of the Spirit of Christ to choose doctrinal subjects rather than the practical. There are many Christless discourses given no more acceptable to God than was the offering of Cain. They are not in harmony with God."[1]

3. *Knowledge without power causes secondary issues to become primary.* The greatest battles in the church I grew up in were over secondary issues: hair length for guys; movie theater attendance; whether jeans were appropriate for church. Long battles. Lively discussions. Always followed by more rules and

less freedom. When we make *everything* a sin, eventually *nothing* is a sin. It seemed to me that the greatest questions of life were left unattended, especially the most important one—how to develop a saving relationship with Jesus Christ. It wasn't until I was a junior in college that I understood that concept, and the knowledge of a loving Savior traveled the toughest eighteen inches in the world, from my head to my heart.

College daze

At seventeen I graduated from high school and left for college. Another strange town, another set of friends. As many students do, I thought I had graduated from church. But God had other plans.

I had always been a good student, with higher than average grades, but that changed when I got to college. In fact, more than one area of my life suffered. I had been used to a list of rules and regulations with no personal relationship with God. When the people who made the rules and enforced the rules were three thousand miles away, disobedience set in. I saw my life suffer in three areas:

1. Education. As I mentioned before, good grades had always been the norm for me. In college my priorities shifted. It was basketball, friends, and girls. I could wake up at the time I wanted, study or go to class if I wanted, and turn in my work if I wanted. The problem was that most of the time I didn't want to. I wanted to be free to do what I wanted. The first semester's grades showed many flags (Fs), and my parents were disappointed and rightly puzzled, wondering about what had happened to their "A" student.

2. Relationships. Without Christ in them, relationships suffer. They're probably some of the first things to be affected.

Since I didn't apply biblical principles to dating, pain followed, not just for the girls I dated but also for me.

3. Religion. I did not have anyone to wake me up Sabbath mornings, and my friends were not waiting for me in Sabbath School; so more often than not, I spent my Sabbaths in bed rather than with a local congregation. I had always been involved in church—singing, acting, speaking—but when my support system went away, so did my involvement. It's not anyone else's fault, however; I could have attended and gotten involved, but I didn't.

Army man

In my second year of college, I made a sudden choice that left even my friends shaking their heads. I joined the army as a chaplain's assistant. Again the patterns were repeated. A new place. New friends. New experiences. It was during that period that my life began to change. I carried a small New Testament in my pocket and started to read the Bible for myself for the first time in my life. I had always said, even in my wild days, that I wanted to become a pastor. It's all I ever thought I would become. I know, you are probably thinking, *What?* But the truth is that God had selected me from before I was born to be in His army.

The army days were a mixed bag. On the one hand, I was meeting God, reading the Word, and going to chapel services, where I sang in the gospel choir. On the other hand, I was dealing with anger that came out in my relationships with my army mates. But God is patient. We are His handiwork, and He works with us at our pace.

Here's a piece of advice for anyone who is struggling right now with this duplicitous lifestyle. Don't give up on your relationship with God. The goal here is growth, not perfection. It's a process, and as long as you are walking in the right direction, you will get there.

Called

After I came back from the army, my life turned around completely. I started theology classes, started to make the right choices in my lifestyle, and I began to see God bringing about the change in me. He changed what I watched. He changed how I treated the opposite sex. He changed the way I spoke. He took away the anger. I made new friends and started to enjoy a new life. It was during this time that I met my wife, got married, got a church, and my life got going. God had called me to be a pastor.

Lessons learned

I learned some things along the way. Keep these in mind as you relate to prodigals and older sons later on in the book. I also hope these lessons can be a benefit to you as you walk with Jesus every day.

1. Life disconnected from the Father is impossible. It's as impossible as running a car without an engine. It might look good on the outside, but it's not going anywhere. Like the phrase says: "You can fool some of the people all the time, and all of the people some of the time, but you can't fool all of the people all the time." The charade will be exposed at some point. It's like trying to fly a kite without a breeze. You can give the appearance of flight while you run. The moment you stop running, the kite will fall. The truth is that we all stop running at some point, and then it all falls down. Well-hidden pornography content is discovered by accident. The lying gets exposed. The period doesn't arrive. The gig might be fun while it lasts, but the music always stops. Whatever follows is never pretty. So don't pretend. Come clean. The Bible calls that repentance. Let God change you from the inside out.

2. A licentious life is unfulfilling. Many of the testimonies I hear about life without Jesus emphasize the fun people had while far from God: the girls or guys, the drugs, the clubs, and the fun. It seems that what people gave up was way better than what they got. Christianity is made to seem like a chore to be endured rather than an experience to be enjoyed. Let me tell you the truth. Yes, there is some truth to the idea that sin is fun. For a while, it can seem like you are enjoying yourself. Oh, the freedom! The truth is that it never lasts. It's only temporary. And the pain that it causes is double the pleasure that it brought. There is no peace. There is little hope. After the boom from the dance floor has ended and the high has worn off, there is no tranquility. Rather, you are left with nothing but despair.

God has shown us a better way. When we realize we were made for His pleasure and created for a purpose, it makes all the difference in the world. That peace and sense of fulfillment is the greatest thing in the world.

3. Friends matter. Who you surround yourself with will determine a great deal of the direction and destiny of your life. In the story of the prodigal son, that young man found no success in any of his relationships. Do you know why? Because we usually surround ourselves with people who are mostly like us, because we attract who we are. So, if you look at your friends and think, "What a bunch of losers!" you might be seeing a reflection of your own character.

Let me suggest three types of relationships you should have:

1. A mentor to learn from
2. A companion to share with
3. A student you can teach

If you are concerned about your friends and worry about cutting ties with them because you don't want to hurt their feelings, don't worry. The moment you start to change, you will attract the right type of friends and will repel the wrong type.

4. Make changes, not excuses. I could point out all the bad things that happened to me, that were done to me, in the church as reasons to stay away from church. As you know, there are some hurtful people in some congregations. Some of the deepest pain I have ever experienced was caused by religious individuals who forgot (or avoided) Jesus' core teachings on love, grace, and true obedience. At the same time, some of my most deeply satisfying, most wonderful experiences have been made possible because of well-functioning Christians. For example, I met my wife, the love of my life, because someone gave Bible studies to her dad and brought her into the church. I have seen the church heal, minister, provide basic necessities, and be the hands and feet of Jesus. I chose intentionally not to dwell on the bad but to rejoice with the good. The bad will always be with us. So will the good. It's my choice what I focus on.

Instead of complaining about all the things the church isn't, you can choose to focus on all the things the church is. Look for the positive, and you will surely find it. Pain is unavoidable, but bitterness is optional. We can't control what happens *to* us. We can control what happens *in* us. Circumstances are often beyond our control, but our attitude is completely up to us. Maybe you have been hurt by the church. Maybe you came looking for support and all you found was indifference. Maybe people spoke behind your back, kicked you when you were down, and didn't lend you a hand. You have a choice. You can hold on to bitterness and unfavorably compare church people to Jesus, or you can start your healing process. It begins by making a conscious choice to forgive the ones who have hurt you. If you need another person to also pray for you as you begin that process, e-mail me and I will do so (rhvidaministries@ gmail.com).

5. *Prodigals can return.* I know because I did. I'm no more special than you. I don't have superpowers or come from special stock. I am just a sinner saved by grace. How does this process happen? Let me share with you two principles to keep in mind that helped me return home:

- My job is not to change people but to bring them closer to the God who can change people. When our focus is on our sins, we end up continuing in them, because we become what we behold. Let's use the exercise illustration. If you look at yourself in the mirror and do not like what you see, you have two options. One, you can concentrate on how fat you are and cry because after two workouts you pretty much look the same. Or you can get to exercising regularly, and by consistently doing that, you can see the fat disappear eventually, and a new you appears. The same goes for spiritual growth. Don't focus your attention on realities but on possibilities. The people who helped me the most were the ones who inspired me instead of judging me.

- Change takes time, so take the time. There are no three-step plans to lose a hundred pounds in one week, and there are no three-step plans to become the second apostle Paul (or Paulette) in one month. It takes more time than that. The problem with sin is just like the problem with gaining weight. Easy on, hard off! That's one reason not to get into bad habits in the first place. It's much easier to deal with a bad habit that you don't have. So be patient with prodigals, whether it is you or someone else. Change will come. God is not done with you yet.

Ready to prepare a party for prodigals? So am I. Let's go.

---

1. Ellen G. White, *The Voice in Speech and Song* (Boise, ID: Pacific Press®, 1988), 342, 343.

PROBLEM

1 ~ Ready

Key idea: We can't force lost people to return home,
but we can be ready when they arrive.

*So he returned home to his father. And while he was still a
long way off, his father saw him coming. Filled with love and
compassion, he ran to his son, embraced him, and kissed him. His
son said to him, "Father, I have sinned against both heaven and
you, and I am no longer worthy of being called your son."*

*But his father said to the servants, "Quick! Bring the finest
robe in the house and put it on him. Get a ring for his finger and
sandals for his feet. And kill the calf we have been fattening. We
must celebrate with a feast, for this son of mine was dead and has
now returned to life. He was lost, but now he is found." So the
party began.*   —Luke 15:20–24, NLT

My wife, daughter, and sister-in-law were driving across
the country from Virginia to Oregon. Partway on their
journey, they stopped in a town for the Sabbath and decided
to attend church there. They pulled into the parking lot with
their rented moving truck, with a car in tow. Nothing says "I'm
from somewhere that is *not* here" like a rented truck! The three
of them were greeted lukewarmly at the door, skated down
the aisle, forced to endure worship by themselves in their own
private pew, and left without being invited to lunch. This was
a medium-sized church next to an academy, a church that

seemed healthy and pretty well attended. Yet the members were oblivious to the fact there were visitors in their midst.

What if, instead of my wife, a lost person had returned to church after a very long time? What if, that day, a family decided to give church "one more try"? What saddens me about this story is that it is not the first time something like that has happened—*to us, to many.*

No one believes they have an anti-guest church. Very few people describe their congregation as cold. I can't imagine that church members purposefully want to send an antisocial message to newcomers. Yet it happens with alarming regularity.

The Bible passage at the beginning of the chapter is dripping with intentionality. One thing is clear about the father. He does not know when the child is returning, but he will not be caught off guard by his return. Notice the wording:

- Father saw him coming
- Finest robe
- Ring
- Sandals
- Fattened calf
- Party

From the reception to the celebration we can glean two principles:

1. Excellence
2. Intentionality

Let's look at each individually.

Excellence

Someone has said that excellence honors God and inspires people. I am concerned about the lack of excellence in many of our religious operations. We seem to not only allow mediocrity, but in some cases we even encourage it.

Case in point: a church member decides that they would like to sing. They have no talent, but that does not seem to be a deterrent. They insist on singing. The time comes for his or her special music. As they sing, the plastic plants in the foyer shrivel, the babies cry, and three cats commit suicide. When they are done, what does the church say? You guessed it. They say "Amen," reinforcing in the singer that mediocrity is acceptable. Contrast that attitude with what Ellen White said:

> A minister should not give out hymns to be sung until it has first been ascertained that they are familiar to those who sing. . . .
>
> Singing is a part of the worship of God, but in the bungling manner in which it is often conducted, it is no credit to the truth, and no honor to God. There should be system and order in this as well as every other part of the Lord's work. Organize a company of the *best singers,* whose voices can lead the congregation, and then let all who will, unite with them. Those who sing should make an effort to sing in harmony; they should devote some time to practice, that they may employ this talent to the glory of God.[1]

According to her, everyone can and should *sing,* but only the best should *lead.* Is that the case in your church? Are the best people in the best positions to best receive the ones God misses the most?

What I often hear when saints justify mediocrity in church goes something like this:

"They're doing it with the best of intentions."

"They have a sincere heart, and that's all that really matters."

"They're spiritual people."

Really? Do you apply that logic to the rest of your life? Do you use a mechanic because he has a good heart, even though he can't tell the difference between a wrench and a screwdriver? Do you eat food by a well-intentioned chef who can't cook? Will you let a heart surgeon who really loves the Lord operate on you even though she hasn't gone to medical school? Will you allow a pilot to take you on your next vacation who can't fly planes although he keeps up with his devotional life and prays an hour every day? He's doing it sincerely, you know! One of the biggest culprits of lack of excellence in the church is signified by these two words: mismatched saints. People are serving outside their area of giftedness. Here are three commonsense recommendations for improving in this area:

1. One hundred versus one. When we have a mismatch, and assuming we have better options sitting in the pews, we often hesitate to make a move because of the fear of hurting the one. What about the other hundred? Who cares for them? What about the guests? It seems unfair to save the one but sacrifice the hundred. Change is seldom easy; if it were, it would be called chocolate. It requires leadership. It's not easy, but it's necessary.

2. Lead. True leadership is taking everyone forward, not keeping everyone happy. Someone has said that the "secret for success I do not know, but the secret for failure is trying to keep everyone happy." I know confrontation is difficult, especially for some pastors, who entered the ministry because they wanted to help people. One of the most dangerous things you can do as a pastor is take away power from someone. It must be done prayerfully, respectfully, and intentionally. (Remember the hundred!)

3. Teach. Every message should be intentional in moving the congregation in these directions:

- Deeper in their relationship with Christ
- Higher in their level of excellence
- Stronger in their unity with each other

Take, for example, worship and singing, which is the part of ministry we are using for illustration in this chapter. Many pastors, because of the hot potato that worship is, stay away from the topic. That would be a mistake. Teach about worship with balance, consistently. Bring experts in. (By experts, I mean people who actually know what they are talking about, not people who make up stuff and use pseudoscience to prove made-up constructs.)

Here is an example of a lesson I taught my worship team and my church. There are four Cs that make an effective worship team.

Character—Anyone can sing. Not everyone can lead worship. It's imperative that the people who lead others to Jesus have a connection with Jesus. Are they perfect? No. Connected, yes.

Competency—Can they sing? Can they hold a note? Do children cry and cats go crazy when they take the microphone? Do people cringe when they see them get up to lead?

Chemistry—I don't know why it is, but worship teams and choirs are fertile ground for drama. Unresolved issues within the worship team will spill over and become a distraction rather than a blessing.

Commitment—Do they show up to practice? Do they take it seriously? Are they willing to make the effort necessary to improve in all areas? Are they divas?

Let's do everything with excellence.

Intentionality

The second principle we see in the story is intentionality. Many words can describe the father's emotions on the day of the return, but "caught by surprise" would not be a phrase we would use for him. The robe had been bought. The calf had been fattened. The ring, sandals, and party planning had already happened. All they needed was for the prodigal to show up!

If we are going to be intentional about helping prodigals as they return home, here are some questions you must consider.

Concerning what we say:

- Do you keep the service positive? Is the Sabbath School director happy about the members who are there or complaining about the ones that aren't?
- Are you prone to speaking "Adventese," or can guests clearly discern and understand?
- When offering time comes around, does the appeal paint a picture of vision and progress, or is it a list of complaints about bills, past dues, and lack of commitment from members? People *give* to, are *attracted* to, and are *inspired* by a positive vision, not a litany of complaints.
- Is Christ the center of every message? Remember

that a preaching emphasis on sin produces sinners. A preaching emphasis on Christ produces Christians. That does not mean we shy away from hard truths, but it does mean we share those truths from the perspective of the gospel and the cross. "Of all professing Christians, Seventh-day Adventists should be foremost in uplifting Christ before the world."[2]

- Is the Second Coming shared as a blessed hope or used as a fear motivator to change behavior? Consider this gem: "The shortness of time is urged as an incentive for us to seek righteousness and to make Christ our friend. *This is not the great motive.* It savors of selfishness. Is it necessary that the terrors of the day of God be held before us to compel us through fear to right action? This ought not to be. *Jesus is attractive.* He is full of love, mercy, and compassion. . . . It is our privilege to have a calm, close, happy walk with Jesus every day we live."[3]

Concerning what they see:

- Is there clear signage? Do they know where bathrooms, children's classrooms, the sanctuary, and the fellowship hall are?
- Are you a friend to clutter? The longer you are in a church, the less you see it. Andy Stanley, in his book *Deep and Wide,* says it best: "The physical environment does more than leave an impression; it sends a message." In many churches the message is: "We aren't expecting guests. What we are doing here is not all that important. We expect somebody to clean up after us. We don't take pride in our church."[4]

Concerning what they encounter:

- Are people invited to church regularly?
- Are you happy they are there?
- What is your specific, intentional strategy to help first-time guests become fully developed followers of Jesus?

When I give lectures and presentations to pastors and church leaders, I often ask that last question. The blank stares and long-winded answers tell me all I need to know. Guests come to your church. They already overcame a hard week, preconceived notions of God and religion, and their fear of the unknown. Do you see them before they see you? I would suggest three simple action steps:

1. Don't smother them. Opening night of an evangelistic series, a woman, well-meaning but completely misguided, shared with guests that if they were going to attend there they would have to give up milk. That qualifies as smothering. Don't.

2. Don't ignore them. People don't like to be ignored. Shake their hands. Provide opportunities in the worship service for people to interact. Have a fellowship meal afterwards. Give them a five-dollar gas card so they can return. Let them know, from the first interaction to the last goodbye, that they are loved.

3. Don't forget them. Send them a postcard, e-mail, or gift. Let them know how valuable they are.

I was sitting in a convention in Seattle at a table with

people I had never met before. We were talking about church and friendliness. A young woman shared how happy she was about the level of friendliness she experiences at her local church. When she shared what church she attends, I was surprised. It was the same church that ignored my wife when she was traveling across the country and visited one Sabbath morning.

We can't force people to come. We can be ready when they do.

RESPONSE

Harold Altamirano, lead pastor for Life Fellowship, a multicultural Adventist congregation in South Florida

What do you think?

Recently, I went to a charity club meeting. It was my first time. I was scared to death. I wasn't sure who was going to be there. All sorts of questions came to my mind. Were they going to pressure me to join or to give money? Would I fit in? Where was I going sit? How should I dress? And so on.

I was also put on the spot, and I felt very uncomfortable. They recited some sort of pledge that I didn't know, so I mumbled through it. They made some insider jokes that most of the regulars understood and laughed at. They shared things they were doing that I knew nothing about. I wanted to be part of the conversation, but I was left out of it. I looked to see who I could relate with, but I could not find anyone. Granted, they were nice. I liked what I heard and commended the purpose of their existence; however, I really needed to find someone to connect with. I totally felt like an outsider. I was nervous and anxious. I couldn't wait for it to be over.

Can you think of an experience like that? How did you feel?

Let's practice excellence and intentionality to help our guests have a better experience. Here are some ideas:

1. Train and launch a "First Impression Team." They will oversee the first-time experience for guests in all the church's environments, such as the parking lot, foyer, and worship space, so that guests will want to come back based on what they experienced their first time.

2. Develop an assimilation system. How do you assimilate someone into the church, from their first visit to becoming an active member of the church? How will you follow up? E-mail, letter, text, call, or visit?

3. Develop an intentional "Next Steps" process for guests. Going to church can be confusing. We want people to connect and grow in Christ. Think of steps, not programs. Let's make it happen by clearing the road and pointing the way.

4. Assign a "Worship Service" director. This person will help with planning and managing the weekly worship service. Think about your guests as you plan Sabbath service so they know that you are expecting them. Excellence takes intentionality. Allow the mission to drive every program and influence every environment of the church. Remember, the church is not a cruise ship but a fishing boat!

Consider these resources:

- Jonathan Malm, *Unwelcome: 50 Ways Churches Drive Away First-Time Visitors* (Center for Church Communication, 2014)
- Mark Waltz, *First Impressions: Creating Wow Experiences in Your Church* (Group, 2013)

- Nelson Searcy, The Assimilation System (http://www.churchleaderinsights.com)
- Nelson Searcy and Jason Hatley, *Engage: A Guide to Creating Life-Transforming Worship Services* (Baker Books, 2011)

Questions

1. How would your church score in the excellence category? From 1–10

2. How would your church score in the intentionality category? From 1–10

3. What is your strategy to connect with guests?

4. Does your church fail more in the "smother them" or "ignore them" category?

5. Who are you praying for right now that they would come back to church?

---

1. Ellen G. White, *Evangelism* (Washington, DC: Review and Herald®, 1946), 506; emphasis added.

2. Ellen G. White, *Gospel Workers* (Washington, DC: Review and Herald®, 1915), 156.

3. Ellen G. White, "Rest for the Weary," *Review and Herald,* August 8, 1881, 89; emphasis added.

4. Andy Stanley, *Deep and Wide: Creating Churches Unchurched People Love to Attend* (Grand Rapids, MI: Zondervan, 2012), 166, 154.

2 ~ Grace

Key idea: Acceptance precedes transformation.

And while he was still a long way off, his father saw him coming. Filled with love and compassion, he ran to his son, embraced him and kissed him. —*Luke 15:20, NLT*

According to a recent survey, less than 70 percent of Adventists worldwide have confident assurance of present salvation.
—*Jerry Moon*[1]

One day, when I was still a kid, a well-intentioned parishioner gave me a bag of green plastic army soldiers. It probably had a hundred of them. Remember them? There was the bazooka one, several that were in the act of running, and all had guns. As a young boy, that was heaven for me. I started playing war immediately! When my parents came home and saw what was happening, it was disappointing to them. They asked me to get some scissors, proceeded to lecture me on the evils of war, and cut off all the guns from the soldiers. They made all of them into medical missionaries and handed me back all the mutilated green figures. They missed one soldier that had a .45 caliber handgun. He proceeded to kill all the medical missionaries. Interestingly, all three brothers in my family joined the armed forces. Sometimes, what you repress, you encourage.

I tell this story to give you a glimpse of the type of atmosphere I grew up in. I'm convinced my parents did the best they could. They loved me and wanted to see me in heaven, and they went about it the best they knew how. Yet, I was introduced to religion but not a relationship. I could recite the eschatological timeline from memory, but I did not have a personal experience with the Person that timeline pointed to. We read in Scripture that the key to conversion and spiritual growth is to have a relationship with a person—Jesus. Our efforts should be dedicated to that end, because when that happens, real transformation takes place.

It seemed that people in my church (and sometimes in my house) were more interested in compliance, even if conversion didn't happen. As long as you looked the part, it was fine. Fear was used as a motivator for change. The problem with that strategy is that it never lasts. Jesus changes us from the inside out, and that takes time. Fear changes the outside behavior temporarily, but grace changes the character permanently. Are we after character transformation or just compliance to the rules? Confusing the source of our salvation with its results can leave a new Christian confused and frustrated.

If we are going to create churches where lost people are attracted to Jesus, where the people that God misses the most feel welcome and encouraged, the first order of business is to understand and live out grace, eliminating self-righteous attitudes that send the message to others: **I > U.** Remember, truth was given as a guide, a map, not a mallet. In order for the good news to be good news to others, it first must be good news to you and me. The good news involves the reality that people grow, change, and are transformed for better in an atmosphere of acceptance and grace. When they get grace or, better yet, when grace gets them, transformation follows. Ellen White puts it this way: "Miserable as he was, the prodigal found hope in the conviction of his father's love. It was that love which was drawing him toward home. So it is the assurance of God's love that constrains the sinner to return to God."[2]

In the story of the prodigal son, grace does three things:

1. Grace allows you to leave your past in the past. Note two interesting items in the prodigal son's attitude as he considered returning home: "So he went and *hired himself out* to a citizen of that country, who sent him to his fields to feed pigs" (Luke 15:15, NIV; emphasis added).

And then note what he planned to say as he returned home. " 'I am no longer worthy to be called your son; *make me like one of your hired servants.*' So he got up and went to his father" (verses 19, 20, NIV; emphasis added).

He was a servant in the strange country. And then he wanted to be a servant in his father's home. Grace says no to that construct. One of the most insidious consequences of graceless religion is that it smuggles your past into your future.

Most of us have things in our past that we are not proud of. A failed relationship. Sleeping with the wrong person. A marriage that ended in disaster. A theft, abuse, abandonment, or addiction. In my most reflective times (usually when I am driving), I think back on my life and regret some of the decisions I made. Isn't it funny that we forget a thousand blessings and have perfect memory of that one failure? If truth be told, I find it harder to forgive myself than to forgive others.

I remember a rainy Friday night, around 10:00 P.M., when my daughter was just five years old. My wife had left to take some teens home after a small-group gathering that took place in my house. A church elder was scheduled to pick me up and take me to a church retreat. When he arrived, my wife was not home yet. He asked me to leave because people were waiting for me. I was *needed* at the camp. So I had a decision to make. I could wait for my wife to get home or leave my daughter by herself for a short while. I chose wrong. I gave Vanessa her blankie, put on a VHS tape of *Veggie Tales,* kissed her, and left. Shortly after, a thunderstorm stuck. Trees moving, wind howling, sideways rain hitting the windows. Lightning. Thunder. My wife was stuck on a road with a fallen tree in front of her for an hour. My daughter was at home alone. To complicate matters, the lights went out. Instead of being held by her father and told everything would be fine, she was alone in a big, empty, scary house. Meanwhile, her father was fulfilling his mission.

My daughter has never forgotten. Sometimes when she asks me for money to go to the mall and I say that I don't have any, she simply says, "Dad, remember when I was five years old . . ." Works every time.

Grace has allowed me to grow from that experience. I don't have to live back there. I can be restored to full sonship, and my past does not have to define me, control me, or destroy me. The song does not say Jesus "paid for some"; it says that "Jesus paid it all." Thanks to grace, the failures from my past can teach me, but they do not have to define me.

2. Grace allows you to celebrate "unfair" blessings. One of the most significant characteristics of a grace-filled Christian is the ability to genuinely rejoice over the successes of other people. As the father stated in Luke 15:23, "And kill the calf we have been fattening. *We must celebrate* with a feast" (NLT; emphasis added).

Grace is not being upset when others have it easier than

you. If it seems unfair, it's because it is! Contrast the attitude of the older son with that of the father. The son screams, "It's not fair!" Yet he forgets that he also was a debtor to the father, that it was his father's riches that allowed him to have an inheritance in the first place.

Allow me to illustrate. Imagine Jesus shows up at your house and tells you that in order to go to heaven, a person must swim from the coast of Florida to Portugal, a trip of about four thousand miles. So people get in the water and start swimming. Some will swim one mile and drown. Some will swim one hundred miles and drown. Some will drown in ten feet of water. At the end of the day, *all drown*. No one makes it to Portugal. Some get far, some go farther, some are farthest, but *all* go far enough to die. We can't make it. We need grace. We need someone to put us on a plane and take us there! That someone is Jesus, and that journey is called grace.

Grace is for all of us, not just for the prodigals. It's for the one who has the intact marriage and the one who has failed. Twice. Grace is for the one who never tasted alcohol and for the one who can still feel its aftertaste after a rough night. For the one who is full of sin and the one full of religion. The ditch on the right. The ditch on the left. They are different ditches, but ditches nevertheless. Grace is for them, and us.

When churches get this, grace destroys the us-versus-them mentality. Churches become more intentional in presenting the gospel in a way that confronts sin but comforts sinners. The gospel does not say that God makes a bad person into a good person—that's moralism. He makes a dead person come alive. That's grace. "Self-righteousness, passed off as holiness, is one of the greatest obstacles to people hearing a loving, grace-filled gospel. Instead of repelling sinners and seekers, Jesus' holiness brought him scandalously close to skeptics, prostitutes, and social rejects. It didn't drive them away."[3]

There are two characteristics of legalists:

- They judge others based on actions but themselves based on intentions.
- They are easy on themselves but hard on others.

Graceful churches are genuinely happy when sinners come back home. They perceive them as welcomed guests, not threats. They are intentional in building bridges and not walls, because they recognize that you can't really embrace someone you are pointing your finger at. It would be wise to remember that the universal symbol of Christianity is a cross, not a ladder. The gospel is good news, not just good advice. It's not us climbing to God, it is God coming down to save us. Heaven is promised to the ones who understand how wretched they are, and how good God is. That's why we can be happy when prodigals return and are received with a party and not stoning. They understand how repentance really works:

It was taught by the Jews that before God's love is extended to the sinner, he must first repent. In their view, repentance is a work by which men earn the favor of Heaven. And it was this thought that led the Pharisees to exclaim in astonishment and anger, "This man receiveth sinners." According to their ideas He should permit none to approach Him but those who had repented. . . . We do not repent in order that God may love us, but He reveals to us His love in order that we may repent.[4]

Graceful Christians understand that before repentance and confession see the Father, forgiveness and compassion see the Son. The order matters.

3. Grace allows you to experience real approval. The son came back home a broken human being. Everyone he had connected with before, expecting to receive approval and affirmation, had failed him. Notice the trail of failed relationships along the way:

He had an older brother who ignored and resented him. "Yet when this son of yours comes back after squandering your money on prostitutes, you celebrate by killing the fattened calf!" (Luke 15:30, NLT). The older brother never calls him "my brother," but instead he uses "your son." Fail.

He had friends who used him. "A few days later this younger son packed all his belongings and moved to a distant land, and there he wasted all his money in wild living" (verse 13, NLT). "Evil companions help him to plunge ever deeper into sin, and he wastes his 'substance with riotous living.' "[5] It's not difficult to see how quickly the friends left him when the money ran out. Fail.

He had an employer who abused him. "He persuaded a local farmer to hire him, and the man sent him into his fields to feed the pigs. The young man became so hungry that even the pods he was feeding the pigs looked good to him. But no one gave him anything" (verses 15, 16, NLT). He was just a number, a servant, no more than a commodity. His boss did not care about the person, just his production level. Fail.

He had a father who saw him. Felt for him. Embraced him. Elevated him. Defended him. "So he returned home to his father. And while he was still a long way off, his father saw him coming. Filled with love and compassion, he ran to his son, embraced him, and kissed him" (verse 20, NLT). Faster are the eyes of the father than the feet of the son. "Never a prayer is offered, however faltering, never a tear is shed, however secret, never a sincere desire after God is cherished, however feeble, but the Spirit of God goes forth to meet it."[6] Win.

True acceptance is found in God, who embraces the sinner and restores the sinner's life so that it produces a transformed disciple.

People are looking for grace. The problem is that grace is hard to find. Where can people find grace in your city? They cannot find grace in the following areas:

- **Sports.** You play well, you get paid. Endorsements, applause, and fans come to the winner. Sports are ruled by performance.
- **Work.** You work well, you get the bonus, promotions, accolades, the corner office, and the raise. Work is ruled by works (no pun intended).
- **School.** You put in the work, do well on your tests, you get on the dean's list. Hard workers usually get the scholarships, the summa cum laude, and the parchment paper on the wall that says to everyone, "I earned this." School is ruled by works.

Our world is ruled by works. From the supermarket to the information superhighway, the principle is the same. You get what you work for, sometimes less. It's impossible to buy a car by grace, or a house, or a computer. If you want to go to the mall, get a bite to eat, or get a haircut, come prepared to pay for it. Credit cards supposedly have a "grace period," but it usually lasts only thirty days and comes with strings attached.

The question remains: If we all have failed, and grace is the solution for that failure, where can we find grace? Where is the place people can experience liberating, transforming, life-changing grace? Once again, one word: *church*. Church is the place for grace. It's the hope of the world. It's the only place where you can see love for the sinner while he or she is overcoming sin. It's the hospital where patients receive treatment and recuperate. It's the place people can come just as they are and leave better than they were. Church, with all its imperfections, can be the vehicle that God uses to help His children learn about His grace. Church is the place God wants real people to come, where He'll reveal real problems and provide real solutions. A place where we can experience grace and love. "Love cannot be commanded; it cannot be won by force or authority. Only by love is love awakened."[7]

The question is, once they come, will they find it?

RESPONSE

Anthony WagenerSmith, lead pastor and church planter of LifeSpring Adventist Church in Tampa, Florida

What do you think?

In my ministry I've seen firsthand the wreckage caused by the absence of grace: prescribing healthy food without feeding on the bread of life; having the "What would Jesus do?" conversation without ever bearing witness to "who Jesus is"; following an unspoken code of holiness without a vital experience of the Holy Spirit; and the commercialization of our outreach while refusing to open our refrigerator to our neighbors.

Yet the key to having grace-filled congregations is to become grace-filled leaders. Our capacity as Christian leaders to experience prodigal/father transformation comes not from self-improvement but self-surrender. Only through Christ can we come to truly know the Father for who He is and ourselves for who we really are.

The story of the prodigal parallels the story of God's grace: he grew up in the family (Creation), lived alone (Fall), was forgiven (Redemption), and was restored to the family (Restoration). To understand my own gospel story, I regularly reflect on these four questions: (1) "Who or what most shaped my life growing up?" (Creation); (2) "How did I first become aware of brokenness in my life?" (Fall); (3) "How has Jesus specifically redeemed me from brokenness?" (Redemption); and (4) "How is He daily restoring me back into wholeness?" (Restoration).

Since I was raised in a highly driven environment, what shaped my life most was the expectation that if I did X, I would get Y. And it worked. I studied hard and got all As; I trained hard and excelled in sports; I practiced hard and received musical opportunities, and on and on. However, the greatest source of human frustration is unfulfilled expectations. The Father brought me in touch with my own brokenness through several situations where doing X did not lead to Y. I was preparing for admission to the U.S. Naval Academy and had a seizure before my first solo flight. I had saved money ever since I was a young kid to buy a house, only to give it back to the bank once the market collapsed.

My unmet expectations produced bitterness, anger, and frustration. For the first time, I saw grace. Unlike me, Jesus became neither prideful when things went well nor bitter when things went south. He always did X, but instead of receiving Y, He received insult, rejection, and ultimately death. Yet through it all, He surrendered Himself to God's will on my behalf (1 Peter 2:23). His grace restores in me the freedom from predetermined expectations, and a life defined not by what I do but what He has done on my behalf.

We desperately need a generation of new leaders who experience radical transformation in the arms of the Father. Only then will we have environments of gospel fluency, speaking less of ourselves and more of His grace.

What do you do?

Here are some of the specific ways I seek to foster grace in my ministry.

Moving from a worship service to service as worship. Church is not a program to attend, it's a community in which God's grace is on display. In the churches I've planted, we developed a rhythm of canceling worship services on a regular basis to show grace in tangible ways in our city. Not only is this a beautiful integration of Sabbath theology, but it provides multiple opportunities for those outside the circle of faith to experience the family of God. Possible ways include renovating public parks, installing new wheelchair ramps for disabled seniors, celebrating the contributions of health-care workers, handing out care packages for university students, eating with the homeless instead of simply serving them a meal. Since seeking the lost includes what we do with them, not merely for them, we intentionally invite those who do not know Jesus to participate with us.

Adopting inclusive language. I want anyone from any background to be able to feel included in the family of God, be they older or younger brothers and sisters. As a result, instead of expecting them to run code, we change our language. From the formal Happy Sabbath and Sabbath School to unexplained talk of unions, divisions, and even AY (would you feel comfortable at something called MY if you were not a Mormon youth?), we speak in ways that foster inclusive community. Our values and theology never change, but our approach must. To use a ranching metaphor, American cattle ranchers start by building fences and spend all their time nurturing cattle on the inside. The cows stick their necks over the fence, always curious about the outside world. By contrast, Australian cattle ranchers don't build a fence around huge swaths of land. They start by digging a well. The cattle have no reason to leave because it is their source of life. Our role as leaders is not to build fences, where the focus is on convincing outsiders to become insiders. Our role is to dig a well where all are invited to journey closer to the living water found in Jesus. The difference is not the cattle; the difference is the environment. And the onus on us as leaders is to create environments of grace.

Challenging the church to reprioritize around seeking the lost. When someone tells me they don't have time to share the gospel, it becomes apparent that the problem is a lack of gospel understanding, not time management. Our greatest need is not to clear our schedules so we can do more "church stuff." What is needed is to live out our already existing rhythms with gospel intentionality. For example, the gospel says God is our Father and we are adopted into His family. If this is true, then the question becomes, "How does your family include others in its rhythms as an opportunity to experience a small taste of what it's like to be included in God's family?" If one of your members works eighty to ninety hours a week, do they at least eat two to three meals a day? If so, that's fourteen to twenty-one meals a week. What if, instead of doing "church stuff," they just intentionally invited a non-Christian to eat with them for one of these meals? Discipleship is not a program to attend or a curriculum to complete. It's about bringing all of Jesus into all of life. We must intentionally live this out as leaders and find ways to celebrate it in the people we serve.

Questions

1. How does a church retain both righteousness and mercy? What practical steps can you do to live this out in your life?

2. How are new, lost people seen in your church? How many are you intentionally connecting with on a regular basis and extending grace to?

3. Every church says they want to reach lost people. What level of "lostness" are you comfortable with?

4. Is the gospel good news to you?

5. Once people come to your church, will they find grace there?

---

1. Jerry Moon, "Ellen G. White on Assurance of Salvation" (course outline, Seventh-day Adventist Theological Seminary, Andrews University, Berrien Springs, MI, 2006).
2. Ellen G. White, *Christ's Object Lessons* (Washington, DC: Review and Herald®, 1941), 202.

3. Jonathan K. Dodson, *The Unbelievable Gospel: Say Something Worth Believing,* Kindle edition (Grand Rapids, MI: Zondervan, 2014), 54.

4. White, *Christ's Object Lessons,* 189.

5. Ibid., 199.

6. Ibid., 206.

7. Ellen G. White, *The Desire of Ages* (Mountain View, CA: Pacific Press®, 1940), 22.

3 ~ Stay

Key idea: Retention is as important as addition.

There was a man who had two sons. The younger one said to his father, "Father, give me my share of the estate." So he divided his property between them.

Not long after that, the younger son got together all he had, set off for a distant country and there squandered his wealth in wild living. . . .

"But when this son of yours who has squandered your property with prostitutes comes home, you kill the fattened calf for him!"

—*Luke 15:11–13, 30, NIV*

The son packed his belongings and left.

Gone.

Just like that.

Just like today.

We lose forty-three out of a hundred.

Let that number sink in for a minute.

Forty-three out of a hundred. Gone.

Let me ask you a question. In what other area of your life is this ratio acceptable?

Would you go to a hospital that had forty-three deaths for every one hundred live births?

Would you dine regularly at a restaurant where forty-three out of one hundred meals gave you diarrhea?

Would you buy a car from a company that for every one hundred cars produced forty-three lemons? (If you own a Kia, we already know the answer.)

Would you let a mechanic fix your car that disabled forty-three out of one hundred cars he touched?

Nowhere in this story do you see the older brother pleading, talking, or interceding with his younger sibling to get him to stay. He never calls him "brother." Not once. He calls him names, he calls out his sins, he calls him "your son," but he never calls him "brother." He let him go with no resistance. How about us? Do we have a problem letting people walk out? Here is a quote that should give us pause: "In this century, the ratio of people lost versus new converts is 43 per 100."[1]

I talk to pastors all the time, and one of the concerns I hear the most can be summarized in what one pastor told me: "Last year I had an evangelistic series. We baptized twenty-five. Of those, one still comes to church. Infrequently."

We have two options before us:

1. Stop doing public evangelism because it's obviously the problem.
2. Understand that evangelism isn't the problem, but the way we do it can be.

I'm going to be pretty blunt in this chapter, and I hope you hear what I am saying and what I am not saying. I have had multiple conversations in more than twenty years of personal experience as a pastor and a pastor's pastor. I do six evangelism meetings a year. I am very concerned about bringing people into the church. I am also very concerned about keeping them in. As we look around America, the prognosis for the church can seem bleak: "According to the *Churchless* data, in the 1990s, 30 percent of the American population was unchurched. Today, two decades later, that percentage has risen to more than four in ten Americans (43 percent)."[2] Millions of people who used to attend church now don't, across all denominations. Ours is no exception. Do lots of people still get baptized? Sure. Do many disconnect after doing so? Regretfully, yes. We can do better. We must.

It all starts with examining a familiar entry point of many into our church. It's called evangelism. I believe that evangelism is like having a baby. If you want to have a healthy baby, three things must happen: conception, pregnancy, delivery.

If you want to produce healthy spiritual babies, the process is seldom completed in one month. There must be an initial connection, a time of gestation, and a smooth delivery done by a person who is more interested in delivering a healthy baby than in winning the MBD (Most Babies Delivered) award.

My personal experience in the process of evangelism in North American churches, except in rare exceptions, goes something like the following:

- We make no friends with unbelievers.
- We schedule an evangelistic series.
- Still no friends or Bible studies.
- We wait for three weeks before the meeting to have the mail carrier do what we ought to do.
- Still no friends.
- We start the meeting, with sporadic support of the church members.
- People come for a month or less, wonder why church members are not there, accept Bible truths, and get

baptized.
- Still no friends.
- A short while later, some leave. Sometimes many.
- We blame the evangelist, the devil, and the new people for not being diligent enough to accomplish in one month what has taken us a lifetime to conquer.
- Rinse and repeat.

When you have conception, pregnancy, and delivery in one month, it's called an abortion. If you are concerned that you have fetuses filling your pews, now you know why. Later on in the book I will share the model I use for evangelism that increases retention rate by 30–40 percent. Still not perfect, but an improvement.

So why do people leave?

- Some leave because they stopped believing in God.
- Some leave because they stopped believing in some or all of the fundamental beliefs.
- Many leave because of conflict, disconnection, and personal struggles.

While the following quote might not be true in every case, it certainly applies to many of the people who have stopped attending church: "Behind every heresy there is a hurt."

Our own data shows a disturbing trend: "Veteran Adventist Church researcher Monte Sahlin said the reasons people drop out of church often have less to do with what the church does and its doctrines than with problems people experience in their personal lives—marital conflict or unemployment, for example."[3]

You have probably heard that in order to stay connected to the church, most people need at least six friends. Most don't have even one—hence the exodus. Great name for a Bible book; not that great for an ecclesiastical reality.

So what are we going to do about it? I ask you to consider the following suggestions. Most of these ideas I have tried myself or seen done in real-life churches, not the imaginary world some church-growth guru made up.

1. Celebration. Every baptism must be celebrated. Only the devil and likeminded individuals get upset when a prodigal comes back home. Since the best reclaiming strategy is to keep the ones we have, I encourage you to do the following:

- Show a video recording of the person's testimony at the baptism. It will remind them in the days to come why they made the decision.
- Give a video and pictures of the baptism itself to the new member.
- Have a banquet for new believers. It can happen quarterly or whenever there is a baptism. There is joy in heaven. Let's join them.

2. Community. We grow better in community. Note the attitude of the older brother and contrast it with the father. One of them ignored and resented. The other celebrated and embraced. Why not try the following?

- Assign a healthy Christian to mentor the new believer. One of the most damaging things that can happen to a new believer is to be blasted with unbalanced materials as they begin their Christian walk.

- Have new-believers class. The minimum time they should be in it is six months. The ideal time is a year. Ground them in Christ. Teach them righteousness by faith. Teach them how to share their faith. Help them know why they believe.
- Visit them at least monthly for the first six months. It's like a marriage. If it passes the first six months without either person quitting, the probability of the couple staying together increases.

3. Connection. I did an evangelistic series in a church in Memphis, Tennessee, and baptized twenty-five people. The board voted that every single one of them was to be involved in some sort of ministry. Some were assigned to be deacons, others to prison ministries, some were given responsibility in small-group leadership or in the children's department (with background check). When new soldiers come to the battlefield, we don't tell them to sit down for a while; we give them a weapon and let them join in. They don't become generals overnight, but telling them to sit on the side of the road and watch others fight can actually be detrimental to their well-being. Do this:

- Assign new believers to specific, gift-based responsibilities.
- If your church has small groups, have them join one. Make sure the leader visits them.
- Have new believers be involved in an evangelistic event—a series, a Revelation seminar, or an outreach event. New people have more unchurched friends they can share their faith with. Don't miss that opportunity.

4. Church. If someone ends up leaving and you want to bring them back, what are you bringing them back to? Is the church ready to receive the prodigals?

Recently, I received a message from a desperate mother. She pleaded with me to speak with her children, who had grown up in the church but were now gone—all three of them. As a parent I can sympathize with her. The worst thing that could happen to me, counting death as an option, is to reach heaven without my kids. It makes me sad just thinking about the possibility. So I understand the pain this mother feels. As I meditated on her request, I became doubly sad. One, because a mother is wanting her children to come back to church. Two, the church is probably not ready to receive them. Why would they go back to that same church with mostly the same people that caused them to leave? The same church that has no relevant worship, that fights about responsibilities, that majors in minors, and that has very few remaining young adults. A church that is more concerned about dress, diet, and drums than about developing a person into a disciple. Infighting. Politics. Legalism. Why in the world would the kids want to go back to the same thing they left? If you are going to be intentional about keeping and reclaiming, the atmosphere and the culture must change. That does not mean you change the doctrines or the biblical principles. It means that the church culture lives out the principle of trying to be as holy as Jesus, but not any holier. When churches forget about the gospel, they start making methods into messiahs. Jesus is attractive.

Churches tend to drift inwardly. It's like walking on a treadmill. If you are not intentional about moving forward, you go backward. There is no standing still. Everything your church does right now is either moving you closer to your goal or keeping you from it.

I have two brothers who are disconnected from the church. It would make me really happy if they decided to return. I had hoped they would never leave, but they did. Why did it happen? What can we learn from the experience of "dones" and "gones"? While you cannot guarantee that all will stay, you can certainly increase the probabilities. Even Jesus lost one, even though He did everything He could to keep Judas.

What can we do this week?

Stop. The problem many times is not that the church members are not friendly. The problem is that we are friendly with ourselves. We have good friends to whom we gravitate and sit next to in worship, talk to at the end, and invite over after church. Stop being friendly with only your friends.

Start. Intentionally (there is that word again) look for people who are new. Engage them in conversation. Sit next to them, introduce yourself, and welcome them. I know you're not in the hospitality committee, but do it anyway. The effect when people greet, smile, and welcome a person is amazing. Even if you don't become BFFs, they will leave with a positive impression.

Say. Say their name. Learn it and say it. Nothing deflates a new member more than to be asked if he or she is a visitor a year after being baptized. Look past the jewelry and makeup or whatever and see the person.

These are not hard things to do. Don't be like the woman I met on a recent preaching assignment. I was visiting a church on a Saturday night. My teenage daughter was with me. (She was in church on a Saturday night. Not at the movies. Not at a sleepover. Not hanging with her crew. She was at church!)

After the two-hour service, a woman approached her and said, "I see that you are wearing makeup. I prefer the natural look." My daughter, without missing a beat, responded, "I don't always wear makeup, only on Sabbaths because it's a special day."

Silence. Don't keep silent. Say nice things to people. Compliment them on their positive traits, on the fact that they are in worship. Resist the urge to criticize or correct all the time. No one died and appointed you Elijah. You are neither a prophet nor the son of a prophet, so relax. Love people for who they are. It's my job to fish them and keep them in the boat. It's God's job to clean them.

Create such a positive experience for believers that, even if they leave, their memories of the Father's house are so overwhelmingly positive that they will have no choice but to return.

A church in the western United States has around ninety members. They have been at ninety members for twenty years, but they baptize people every year. Something is not right—that math does not add up. When I inquired as to why, the reason became obvious pretty quickly. Let me explain.

The church started a food bank. Wednesday-night prayer meeting tripled because guests were coming for the food but staying for the service. Several people in the church complained. They said things such as, "Who are these new people? Who invited them? They won't take good care of God's house." The pastor started a Christmas tradition of a banquet for the community. More than a hundred guests came. On the third year, the board sat him down and said, "Pastor, for the last two years you have done a Christmas banquet for the community. When are you going to do one for us?" One of the newcomers offered to start a community choir to do Christmas carols. He was a professional choir director in his country. The response from the music leader in the church was, "That is bringing strange fire into the house of God. He is not Adventist." She felt threatened, not happy. Sound familiar? I wish this were an isolated incident. It isn't.

I am asking you to take an honest look at your church and remind yourself and your people why it is that you exist. New people stay, or return, to healthy churches. Remind yourself at least once a day that your job is not to coddle the ninety-nine, to be satisfied with the nine, or to be content just because at least one of the sons is still home. Every life matters, and lost people matter to God. Do they matter to you?

RESPONSE

Richie Halversen, lead pastor of College Drive Seventh-day Adventist Church in Jackson, Mississippi, and church planter of a new congregation in the same city

What do you think?

The overarching theme to this chapter is that "truth" may get people into the church, but only love will keep them. People need to be loved. This has to start with the pastor and percolate into the entire membership. People need to feel needed. This chapter is so important because it is one of the greatest challenges in the church.

The older brother analogy is perfect because it illustrates how we often respond to newly converted, marginal, or lost people. "Pastor, I don't understand how anyone could leave the church after embracing the Sabbath." I would be a rich man if I had a nickel for every time I've heard that one. I've heard members and pastors alike say it. What we don't realize is that when we say that, we're like the older brother in the prodigal story. We're shaking our heads, thinking, *They should've known better.* It's actually us who should know better. "They made their bed, now let them sleep in it," we say. Aren't you glad God didn't say that about saving you? People need to be loved with the type of love with which Christ loved people. Christ loved people with the type of love that said, "I will die for you."

John 15:13 says, "Greater love has no one than this, that someone lay down his life for his friends" (ESV). Often when we hear this verse we rush to extremes. We think of ourselves taking a bullet for a friend (and it does mean that). However, this verse is applicable on a much more practical level. Essentially, our life is made up of what? Time. Our life is made up of seconds, which make up minutes, which make up hours, which make up days, which make up weeks, and so on. Our time is our life. Therefore, when I *give my time* to someone, I am essentially giving him or her my life. I am doing what John said is the greatest kind of love: *I am laying down my life for someone.* This, in its essence, is how we hold on to members; we love them enough to give them our time. This is what I received from this chapter. We have to be intentional about loving people.

What do you do?

Matthew 28:19 says, "Therefore go and make disciples of all nations, baptizing them in the name of the Father and of the Son and of the Holy Spirit" (NIV). Often when I hear the gospel commission, the emphasis is placed on "go." But if you look at the Greek words, the imperative is not "go" but "disciples." In our "go"-ing we forget that our number-one objective is not to fill pews with members but to fill the world with disciples. Disciple making will lead to more bodies in the pews undoubtedly, because disciples make disciples, who make disciples. The reason we've had better retention than many other denominations is that we take discipleship very seriously.

Often we don't do evangelism and discipleship because it takes so much of our time. However, if we're going to grow the kingdom of God, we must recognize that all of our time belongs to God anyway. Here are a few of the ways we have members become disciples—and hold on to them in the process.

1. Consistent evangelism. We have to stop thinking of evangelism as something we do and start seeing it as something we are. There is nothing wrong with event evangelism; after all, the Day of Pentecost was event evangelism. However, public evangelism is just one event in the ecosystem of evangelism. In drug recovery we say, "You can't keep what you have without giving it away." We know that if the addict does not get involved with service work, they will go back to their old life. The same goes for the sinner. When we do consistent evangelism, we continually create opportunities to plug people into service positions. Whenever we have a new reaping series, the people who joined during the last reaping series lead out in this series. These same people will train the new people in the next series. This is an intentional way of forcing yourself, and your church, to plug new people into service. And while they're serving, they're building relationships.

2. Agape feast. After each reaping series, we always have an agape feast to celebrate the new members and their decision for Christ. We celebrate the Lord's Supper together in a warm, inviting, less formal environment. The tables are filled with fresh fruit, breads, and candlelight. This is another intentional way we build relations.

3. Visitors' lunch/home invitations. Every Sabbath we have a visitors' lunch. We do not single out visitors or make them go, but just having it available lets them know they're important. I also make sure new members are invited to different homes for Sabbath lunch over the course of the next three months after joining. Does this take time? Yes. Should people do this naturally? Yes. But do they? No. This is where discipleship comes in.

4. Spontaneous discipleship. I had a series of meetings where I baptized four millennials (yes, traditional evangelism, rightly done, will reach them). These four young people were hungry to study the Word. I knew if I didn't do something different, we wouldn't hold them. So we started a new small group at a coffee shop on Sundays at 11:00 A.M. I needed to be there in the beginning to let them know I cared and to help get it off the ground. The meeting is still going every Sunday and growing, whether I'm there or not.

The bottom line is that church is, and will always be, about the people. We are called to make disciples of people. Discipleship takes time. But nothing says "I love you" like giving someone your time. This is my number one problem with hiring musicians in the church. I am not saying that it is never appropriate, it's just that it usually compromises discipleship. It's much easier to hire someone than to make a disciple of someone. But the gospel commission says make disciples, not hire them. If I am not allowing someone to use their God-given talents just because they don't quite do it well enough, for the sake of my program, I am compromising the gospel commission.

People will always be more important than programs. If people feel that from the pulpit to the pew, they will stay.

Questions

1. How successful is your church at keeping new believers?

2. Which of the practical suggestions are you already doing? Which ones will you implement? How? When?

3. When someone goes around criticizing new believers, it's the job of the rest of the body to confront the accuser of the brethren. What systems are in place in your local church to make sure new people are assigned healthy mentors?

4. How soon are new people put to work in your church after they are baptized?

5. Is your church ready to welcome back the prodigals? Are you?

---

1. Ansel Oliver, "At First Retention Summit, Leaders Look at Reality of Church Exodus," Adventist News Network, November 19, 2013, accessed November 23, 2015, http://news.adventist.org/en/all-news/news/go/2013 -11-19/at-first-retention-summit-leaders-look-at-reality-of-church-exodus.

2. "George Barna & David Kinnaman on the Rise of the Churchless," Barna Group, January 8, 2015, accessed November 23, 2015, https://www .barna.org/barna-update/culture/702-george-barna-david-kinnaman-on -the-rise-of-the-churchless.

3. Oliver, "At First Retention Summit."

4 ~ Conflict

Key idea: Treat antagonists with respect, but don't stop the party.

The older brother became angry and refused to go in. So his father went out and pleaded with him. But he answered his father, "Look! All these years I've been slaving for you and never disobeyed your orders. Yet you never gave me even a young goat so I could celebrate with my friends." —Luke 15:28, 29, NIV

It's amazing what people will fight about in church. Most church "fights" I experienced as a pastor had nothing to do with preservation of doctrinal purity or concern for missional direction. Instead, they were usually about such earth-shattering problems such as the following:

- Who had the keys to the kitchen?
- Who used the kitchen and left it dirty?
- Who was allowed to use the kitchen in the first place? (Notice a trend here?)

A chapter on conflict resolution in a book about church growth and evangelism might seem out of place. The reason I decided to put it in is that church conflict is probably the greatest hindrance to congregations deciding to do evangelism, and it acts as missional kryptonite. We all fight. All churches do. Conflict denotes passion, and that is preferable to apathy.

Churches that are not missional fight more and dirtier, and about less important things. Let me share a study from Thom Rainer about this topic:

In our survey we found ten dominant behavior patterns of members in these churches. Three of them are especially significant. See if you recognize these in your church:

1. *Worship wars.* One or more factions in the church want the music just the way they like it. Any deviation is met with anger and demands for change. The order of service must remain constant. Certain instrumentation is required while others are prohibited.
2. *Prolonged minutia meetings.*
3. *Facility focus.* The church facilities develop iconic status. One of the highest priorities in the church is the protection and preservation of rooms, furniture, and other visible parts of the church's buildings and grounds.
4. *Program driven.* Every church has programs even if they don't admit it. When we start doing a ministry a certain way, it takes on programmatic status. The problem is not with programs. The problem develops when the program becomes an end instead of a means to greater ministry.
5. *Inwardly focused budget.*
6. *Inordinate demands for pastoral care.*
7. *Attitudes of entitlement.*
8. *Greater concern about change than the gospel.* Almost any noticeable changes in the church evoke the ire of many; but those same passions are not evident about

participating in the work of the gospel to change lives.
9. *Anger and hostility.*
10. But the biggest one is:
11. *Evangelistic apathy.* Very few members share their faith on a regular basis. More are concerned about their own needs rather than the greatest eternal needs of the world and community in which they live.

In almost every behavior above, church members were looking out for their own needs and preferences. I want the music my way. I want the building my way. I am upset because the pastor didn't visit me. I don't want to change anything in my church.

You get the picture. I. Me. Myself.[1]

A friend of mine likes to say that if you don't believe the devil exists, try doing some evangelism. Any church that decides to be more evangelistically minded will catch some heat. We expect it to come from outside the church, but it is very discouraging to hear church members downplay, resist, and even attack missional efforts. I am more concerned about the apathy and antagonism inside the church than about the atheists outside of it. It is of paramount importance that you accept the fact that antagonists are part of the deal. Here are five "you wills" that you must remember:

- You will be attacked. Expect it. Endure it.
- You will be dismissed. Some will listen to what you have to say and dismiss you.
- You will be ignored. Some will not even listen to your vision.

- You will be talked about. Some will gossip, make up stories, write letters, and have secret meetings.
- You will be blessed. After every challenge, God will turn your test into a testimony of His power. As you look back, it will become clear how God led.

The question you have to ask yourself when going through church turbulence is this: Is it worth it? I am praying your answer will be yes. In the story of the prodigal son, the older brother stays outside, angry (the word there signifies deep-seated wrath) and resentful. The father is respectful toward him, but he does not tell the band to stop playing or put the food away or end the celebration.

In this chapter I would like to share with you five principles concerning antagonists.

1. If you don't want to be attacked, ask God not to bless you. Whatever God blesses, the devil attacks. If you read Scripture closely, you will sense a blueprint in most biblical characters that contains three stages:

- *Promise:* God delivers a promise, a future that is better than the present. This produces encouragement and expectation.
- *Problem:* the promise is immediately followed by a problem. This produces anxiety, maybe some doubt, and certainly pain.
- *Provision:* God delivers on His promise. Sometimes it takes days, and other times years, but He always comes through. The more significant the provision, the more daunting the problem.

Now take any Bible character and you will see that blueprint in their life. David, Esther, Joseph, Abraham, Ruth, Jesus. Another way of saying it is: message, mess, miracle. Every person in the history of the world who did anything significant met resistance at first. No one ever said to a leader who came up with new ideas, "You mean you want to fundamentally change everything we do around here? Sure, go right ahead." That never happens in real life or in church life. Elbert Hubbard was right on this: "Do nothing, say nothing, and be nothing, and you'll never be criticized."

2. Antagonists don't set the agenda. People with a critical spirit are usually not very emotionally mature individuals. They have as much power as you give them. I don't know how many church leaders (pastors and laypeople) have shared with me their frustration with one leader or pastor who wants everything a certain way even though it is not moving the church in a missional direction. It's time that you take a stand and tell serial criticizers, "You don't get to set the agenda." You don't need to reply to every e-mail or answer every call. You don't need to be hurt by every comment or deterred by every opposition. If you wait for everyone to get on the bus, it will never leave the station! Our mission is clear, and our methods must change and improve to become more effective in achieving our mission.

The problem with serial antagonists is threefold:

- They are never satisfied. You will change one thing, and they always look for another.
- They are usually fighting an internal problem that is greater than the one they are attacking. It has been my experience that whenever someone is constantly

67

pointing out faults in others, they are hiding a similar, much greater problem.
- They make you chase the devil's rabbits. A distracted
church is an unfocused church. Chase after souls, not
rabbits.

Ask yourself two questions:

- Who sets your agenda? Since the church does not
have a mission but the mission has a church, the
agenda is already laid out for us. We follow God's
agenda; we do not make our own.
- Who are you empowering? One of the places that I
see the most division is on the Internet. People who,
in person, are sweet and pleasant get behind a keyboard and cut deeply. I had one such person among
my friends on Facebook. Every comment he did not
like on my wall he criticized. He made smart remarks
and accusations. I tried to play nice, responding and
trying to explain myself. It was never enough. So
I did with him what I recommend you do with all
Internet trolls. Remember these four words:

> UNFRIEND
> BLOCK
> REPORT
> DELETE

3. Discover what you are fighting about and why. It seems
that behind many of the conflicts we have in churches are the
following assumptions:

- Anything that you came into the church with is natural and holy.
- Anything that begins or changes after you have been in the church for a while is compromise, unholy, and part of the Jesuit infiltration.

We don't like change. I've said before that one of the advantages our pioneers had over us is that they ministered based on imagination and not memory. Change is hard but necessary. I am not talking about changing the day we worship on. The fundamental biblical principles are unchanging. I am saying we can't upgrade to the level of principle any items that are just personal preference or cultural in nature. Here are some examples:

- Wearing pants to church (for women)
- Telling the food bank director not to include eggs and dairy in the food baskets
- Refusing to serve turkey sandwiches to the homeless
- Telling a story of the loaves and fishes for children's story and avoiding the fish part because you prefer a vegan diet
- Clapping (ever been at a black church?)
- Percussion—yes, we can hear it but not see it
- For or against the ordaining of women

Those are just some of the examples of issues we fight about. I have always found it helpful to be informed with good, balanced material that I can share with sincere antagonists who want the best for the church but are resistant to change because they have never experienced anything different.

Remember: in the essentials, unity. In the nonessentials, liberty. In everything, love.

4. Your job is to be faithful. God's job is to make sure justice is done. Don't defend yourself. When I was starting out in ministry, I sought out Pastor José Rojas for advice. He told me something I have never forgotten and have tried to live by. He said, "Be like Jesus and don't defend yourself." I have tried to follow that advice, with different degrees of success. Think about it. Constantly defending yourself is a waste of time. Your friends don't need it, and your enemies don't believe it.

- Don't fight back. The temptation is to trade fire with fire. Be the bigger man or woman. Love instead. Wash the feet of your antagonists. Don't be a pushover, but don't get in the mud. Engaging antagonists on their level is like wrestling with a pig. You both get dirty, and the pig likes it.
- Don't sit idle. Another negative response to antagonism is to become paralyzed about anything and everything, second-guessing yourself and super-analyzing everything you do to the point of paralysis. You may have to slow down, but keep on moving.
- Don't be afraid. Remember this: If God is for you, those who are against you are wasting their time.

5. Use practical responses to conflict. Since conflict is inevitable, here are four tips for conflict resolution:

- Ask. Don't interpret, assume, or take anything for granted. Don't read into anything or guess. Ask.
- Pray before confronting. (We end fights the way we

start them.) Prayer in the beginning defuses and acts as a wet blanket on a fire that could be about to get bigger.

- Focus. Stick to the real problem, and stick to one problem at a time. Resist the temptation to try and solve other problems. This requires discipline. Also, many times what you think is the problem is not really the problem. Peel the layers and go to the root.

When I was young and living with my parents, we sometimes had company over to our house. It was interesting what happened before and during their visit. The house got cleaned, and we were on our best behavior (well, maybe better behavior). The same thing happens in churches. When the mission gets higher priority, conflicts tend to decrease after a while. The amount of unhealthy conflict in a church is inversely proportional to the mission focus of that church. Usually, the ones who do the least demand the most. The goal, then, should not be for the leader to continually play the "firefighter" role but to keep the church's mission constantly before the people. The more people are involved in the purpose of the church, the less the petty arguments and crazy fights will occur.

- Love. Do you love them? Do you want them to be in heaven? Do you fight like them?

Let me finish this chapter with a real-life situation. A church in a metropolitan area was getting ready to plant a church to reach second- and third-generation Hispanics. The young people in that church got organized, and the church plant was launched. But the resistance to the new church was swift and relentless. Letters were written, anonymously of course. Secret meetings were held. I received calls and reports that were blatantly and absolutely not true. The level of antagonism got so high that I personally questioned the decision to plant a church. One question kept me going. *Is it worth it?* Twenty years from now, will we look at a healthy, vibrant congregation and tell ourselves it was worth it? All the drama, the upsetting phone calls, the vicious e-mails and secret complots. The answer was always *Yes, it is worth it.* That church has more than one hundred people now, many of them professional young adults who are reaching one of the most secular cities in America, and they themselves are planning to plant another congregation.

I share this story to encourage you. If you make God's mission your mission, you will look back and say it was worth it. Maybe not here on earth, but definitely in heaven. Keep throwing parties for prodigals. Don't be deterred by antagonists. "Though you will not join in the greeting to the lost, the joy will go on."[2]

So my challenge to you is . . .

Party on.

RESPONSE

Myron Edmonds, lead pastor and visionary of Glenville Seventh-day Adventist Church in Cleveland, Ohio

What do you think?

This chapter clearly exposes the source of missional impotence in many Seventh-day Adventist churches—conflict. There is nothing wrong with conflict. The best relationships experience conflict. Church is no different, especially with a mission so great as making disciples of the entire world. However, this chapter points out that an over-preoccupation with nonessentials can stall the forward movement of the church.

Pastors and leaders must have the proper perspective as it relates to conflict. Conflict for the leader is often confirmation that they are pursuing a noble endeavor. When you are trying to change people's lives, many times you will have to adapt and change your delivery method in order to be effective. The process of change is what often causes the most vicious conflict. I learned that as a leader you must have a laser focus on the destination of the salvation of souls. You cannot let the grumbling and the attacks of members who are afraid of change dissuade you from the mission.

One way to remain focused is to think in the future versus the now. If you will remain focused on the reason for the mission, the minutia will grow strangely dim in the light of the salvation of souls. This also means that as a leader I cannot take things personally or retaliate when I'm being attacked. When I become preoccupied with the fires in the church, I am yielding to Satan's ultimate plan of distraction from accomplishing the mission. This does not mean to run from conflict. It simply means that I should not allow conflict to transform me into a glorified babysitter instead of a disciple maker.

I especially could relate to the three Ps blueprint in the lives of all great people in the Bible: (1) promise, (2) problem, and (3) provision. The lesson in this threefold guide for the plans of God is that with every promise come both problems and provision. Conflict and problems when pursuing the mission of the church are to be expected. They're par for the course. I should not allow myself to doubt God's vision or my calling just because I experience problems and setbacks, even the most extreme ones. These are reminders that provision is on the way. Somebody's life is going to be changed. A blessing is coming. The leader chooses to remain focused on the mission as the solution to distracting conflicts and antagonistic people.

My personal experience has been that with new levels come new devils. Anytime God gave me an idea and a vision that involved the saving of lives, there was always a challenge equal to it, designed by God to increase my prayer life and faith and designed by Satan to decrease my prayer life and my faith.

What do you do?

1. Keep evangelism going year round. If evangelism and mission are the prime reasons for the existence of the church and the best solution for distracting conflicts, then planning evangelism should not be an annual event but a daily process in the life of the church. For me this means

- making our Sabbath worship services evangelistic;
- making our small groups evangelistic;
- making board meetings and business meetings evangelism focused.

Many pastors I talk to spend most of the year in their churches doing "in-reach." They're trying to "get the church right." This kind of insular thinking is a never-ending cycle. The only thing that will get the church right is to focus it on its mission, not once a year but all the time. You must be stubborn about it. Intense about it. Redundant about it. Souls. Souls. Souls. Never take a break or a hiatus from changed lives, or else it will be the death of the church. In a practical sense, this means that we will do three major things at our church, and they will all have an evangelistic focus: worship, fellowship, and outreach.

2. Keep the church praying. When you have lofty aspirations to change a community, city, or demographic group, you quickly learn it can't be done by human might or power but only by the Spirit of the Lord. Soul winning and evangelism are totally spiritual and supernatural. So then prayer becomes the most important asset you have in making the vision a reality. The more the church prays, the more souls come to Jesus. The less the church prays, the more they prey on each other.

I have discovered that you can tell what Satan is afraid of by what he tries to keep you from doing. The devil doesn't mind the church meeting and greeting and eating and worshiping, but have you noticed how he tries to keep the church too busy to pray? Prayer should be the oxygen in the atmosphere of the church, because the plans are so big that the church realizes their utter dependence upon God, and so they are constantly in a state of crying out to God for His miraculous provision. Practically speaking, this is what I do:

- Appoint a prayer leader who organizes the church into prayer teams.
- Have prayer meetings three times a day via conference call.
- Have prayer meeting once a week with the elders via conference call on Sabbath morning, praying for the services.
- Have quarterly all-night or late-night prayer services, where we spend concentrated time praying for upcoming evangelistic endeavors.

- Have yearly prayer retreats.
- Our worship team prays every Thursday night in preparation for Sabbath service.
- I personally dedicate every Monday as a day of prayer and fasting. I have my assistant clear my schedule. I inform the congregation not to disturb me on Mondays while I am at the church in my office from 9:00 A.M. to 2:00 P.M., seeking God in prayer for the church and asking guidance for vision and mission and understanding in the Word.

3. Outreach every Sabbath. For many years I did outreach every fourth Sabbath of the month immediately after church, but we have since upped the ante and do it four times a month after church for ninety minutes. This has caused us to simplify our Sabbath services, making them more visitor friendly. It also connects what we do on Sabbath morning with outreach. If all we did was have services and no outreach afterward, it would be the equivalent of eating and never having a bowel movement—spiritual constipation. Outreach every Sabbath gives the church a reason for being. We know every week we are going to do something to connect with the community, even if it is a small group. The goal of the leader is not to win the souls but to put the membership in the position to win the souls.

4. Develop leaders instead of whiners. I see myself not as a quarterback but rather a coach. The quarterback runs the plays. The coach designs and calls the plays for the players. Pastors are coaches. Our job is not to run the plays but to put the membership in the best position based on their gifts to run plays for God.

I spend at least two times a month with my elders and other leaders in leadership development exercises. These exercises are designed to make them more effective missionaries in their communities. When we meet, we don't talk about the issues of the church; we talk about how to change the world. This focus on developing disciples who make disciples has increased the clarity of the vision and the support of the vision. In order to remain mission focused, you have to spend the majority of the time with your leaders rather than the entire church. Pouring into the key leaders is the most effective way of pouring into the entire church.

Questions

1. In what areas are you encountering fierce opposition?

2. What resources can you share with your congregation that can help them grow in the areas in disagreement?

3. Of the ten areas of disagreement that the chapter mentioned, which are the top three in your church? Have you seen any improvement in the last year? Why?

4. How difficult is it not to respond in kind when attacked?

5. What antagonist do you need to pray for right now? Do it . . .

---

1. Thom S. Rainer, *I Am a Church Member: Discovering the Attitude That*

Makes a Difference, Kindle edition (Nashville, TN: B&H Publishing Group, 2013), 36–38.

2. White, *Christ's Object Lessons,* 211.

PLAN

5 ~ Pray

Key idea: Prayer is not the preparation for the battle;
prayer is the battle.

When he finally came to his senses, he said, "How many of my father's hired servants have food to spare, and here I am starving to death! I will set out and go back to my father and say to him: Father, I have sinned against heaven and against you. I am no longer worthy to be called your son; make me like one of your hired servants."
—*Luke 15:17–19, NIV*

Prayer can help people come to their senses. It does not guarantee that they will return home, but it makes it easier to return to their Father's house.

Even though I am in my forties, I have seen several trends in the Christian world come and go. Purpose-driven Life, Seeker Movement, and Natural Church Development are just some examples. Churches are constantly asking themselves, How can our church grow? In response to that question, I would ask another question. Why are you asking the wrong question? The right question is, What is hindering my church from growing? It is as important to ask yourself how to reach prodigals as it is to understand what is keeping them far from the Father's house. I believe Mark 3:13–16 gives us some keen insight about the relationship between Christ and His followers and how that affects their ministry. "Jesus went up on a mountainside. He called for certain people to come to him, and they came. He appointed 12 of them so that they would be with him. He would also send them out to preach. And he gave them authority to drive out demons. So Jesus appointed the 12 disciples" (NIrV).

That passage reminds us of three things about communion with God.

1. Prayer reminds us about who called us. The Person who calls you is important! Jesus called His disciples two thousand years ago, and He calls His disciples still. Churches that reach prodigals are clear on their call. They understand that in order for you to get where you are going, you need to know where you come from. A sense of call is especially important during difficult times, because sometimes all you have is your call. When there is no visible manifestation of success, when another nightfall brings with it no news of the prodigal, your call will sustain you. It will sustain you through

- periods of hard economic times;
- people who are hard to deal with (you know who I'm talking about);
- volunteers who won't;
- staff who can't;
- members who shouldn't but do.

Like a seed planted in the soil, results are often not immediate or visible. One of my friends works in a conference with a country church that has one person in attendance. One! What drives that pastor to prepare a message for that one person? His call. In another conference, a church was visited by a conference representative. That particular Sabbath, there was one person in attendance. The man from the conference was preaching his heart out when the member excused himself to go to the bathroom. A short time later the member returned and the sermon continued. These are extreme cases, but the point is this: sooner or later you will experience hard times. When those tough times come, it is imperative that you understand clearly who called you.

When I had only four years of ministerial experience (back when I knew everything), I was asked to help a small congregation while I was doing graduate studies. The first day I was there, we had eight people present. The woman directing Sabbath School would say the welcome, sit down, do the mission story, sit down, and so forth. I don't know if she was trying to give the illusion that more people were present, but it didn't work. The church was far away from our home, extremely cold, the basement sometimes flooded, it smelled bad, and we only had one visitor and ten members.

Our strategy was simple. We had tried everything with no prayer, and *nothing* worked. We decided to stop doing everything and *just* pray. After several weeks we began to work again, and *everything* worked. We went around door to door telling people we prayed for their needs and concerns every week at that small church. The first time a visitor walked into church on Sabbath morning we freaked out because we weren't expecting anyone. She asked us if this was a church and whether we met for services. We tried our hardest to contain our excitement in order to not creep her out!

This happened in a town that sits in the midst of a large fruit orchard, has one traffic light, and most people who lived there came and went according to the harvest. Even though it was hard to get up some Sabbaths, we saw God work there. I was only there for a short time, but I experienced the power of God as I have in very few places I have been. The lesson learned in those hard, cold winter months was very simple. God is working everywhere. We saw drug addicts converted, estranged families reconciled, and an active youth group established. God is at work even when you don't see it. He did not call you to fail. Prayer makes it possible for you to connect with the Person who called you. Remember that God can do for the prodigal in the far country what you cannot. You might not be with him or her, but God is. You can't knock sense into them, but God can.

All the seminary teaching in the universe can't help you if you forget the "who" before starting the "what." Not much happens if you only pray, but nothing happens if you don't pray. That's why we pray to ask God to tell us His plan, not to bless the ones we come up with all by ourselves.

2. Prayer reminds us why He called us. The purpose of His call is important. Notice the three things the disciples were able to do after their call: cast out demons, preach, and heal.

Successful, sustainable ministry is always birthed out of prayer. Before we talk to prodigals about God, we need to talk to God about prodigals!

Sometimes in modern, statistics-driven Christianity, the real purpose that Jesus called us for gets lost. He called us *to be with Him.* From the time of Creation until the end of time, God is fueled by a deep desire to be with the members of the human race. In case you forgot, God is madly in love with you. The whole purpose of your creation was not just that you spend time doing work *for* Him but that you spend time *with* Him. Do you remember how it felt to spend time with someone you were head over heels about? Remember the anticipation? The expectation? The satisfaction when your time was over?

Pastor Alejandro Bullón tells of an older woman who approached him after a sermon. She pointed to a graying gentleman and said, "You see that man over there? He is my husband of forty years. I have never loved him." How tragic. Living with someone you don't love has to rank highest in the "I hope it never happens to me" category. Think about it. The woman in the story was a good wife. She never cheated on her husband. She took the time to prepare meals for him. She ironed his shirts so that he looked good. She entertained guests on special occasions. She went on vacations and celebrated birthdays with him. Yet a key component was missing. She did not love him.

Could the same thing be happening to us? Are we too busy trying to preach impressive sermons about Him, bringing healing to many homes for Him, even working to cast out the evil in society in His name, yet our personal relationship with God is lacking?

Another time, I sat down with Pastor Bullón and three conference administrators, and they asked him about the secret of his evangelistic success. He said, "We teach church members to pray, read their Bibles, and share their faith." They had a hard time with the first two. It seemed too simple. Praying for the prodigals is not the only thing we can do, but it is certainly the most important thing.

I keep a list of prodigals in my life. I routinely pray and fast for them. Some have come home. Some are on their way. Some are still living it up in the far country. My prayers are not determined by their level of closeness to the house. I pray because lost people matter to God. He has called me *to be with Him* before I can reach others for Him.

3. Prayer reminds us that He has called others *too.* The *personality* of those He called with you is important. When we pray, we see the face of God and realize that He can use people whom we don't see eye to eye with. A close look at the personality of the disciples reveals anything but uniformity. They were diverse, and that was a good thing. Different backgrounds. Different social statuses. Different politics. Different jobs. Blue collar and white collar. A Hebrew revolutionary and a Roman sympathizer. One who had a questioning mind, one who spoke too quickly, and one who hardly spoke. Some who were more interested in position than preaching, and one who was constantly taking a piece of the pie for himself. What message was Jesus trying to send us through the selection of His disciples?

If we are going to reach prodigals, we must accept the fact that diversity is not our enemy. Doing ministry alongside people of different backgrounds, races, and economic statuses reminds me of Noah's ark. The similarities to a congregation are plentiful. You can probably relate this to people in your own church:

- The ark was not the most comfortable of places. Other than the obvious living conditions with animals, the ark had many features that kept the comfort level low. It had only one window, and it housed married couples and their in-laws for an extended period of time. It probably didn't have pizza delivery, hot showers, and spacious rooms. Close quarters can bring out the worst in people. I am sure that even though Noah's faith was strong, a lot of questions went through his mind as he looked outside and saw his former home covered with water.

Ministry to people has its great days, but it also has its rainy, depressing, run-of-the-mill days. Reaching prodigals is hard! Managing egos, dealing with childish attitudes, having difficult conversations with sensitive people, and being watchful of extremist tendencies on both sides of the theological road can make for some uncomfortable days.

- The ark was not the cleanest place. Imagine cleaning up for thousands of animals every day for more than a hundred days. The smell would be enough to knock you out. There was animal hair, secretions, and odors aplenty. The church is also not the cleanest place. A long time ago I learned a short poem that goes like this:

> Living in heaven, with saints we don't know,
>   that would be glory.
> Living on earth, with saints we know,
>   well, that's another story.

Ministry is messy. People don't always come through or stay faithful or truthful. Planning can sometimes seem like a play diagramed by the coach on the blackboard that fails miserably when tried on the field. Adjustments have to be made, personnel must be upgraded, and different options need to be looked at. I cringe when I hear people saying that if you implement "these three easy principles," you will have the church you are looking for. It is never that easy. Doing church would be awesome if it weren't for the people!

Case in point. A prodigal comes home, is getting

baptized, and you are celebrating. Then you see "her." While everyone else is happy, she has a scowl. You know you will have a difficult conversation again, for the umpteenth time, about "the people you are bringing into this church." No one said it would be easy. God did say it would be worth it.

- The ark was not the most popular mission project. Only seven people responded to Noah's call to come into the ark. Even though the ark was well known, the call got no response. The more time passes, the less popular the church has become. In a previous chapter, we discussed how attitudes toward the church have shifted. We do not live in a Christian nation. We actually live in one of the most unchurched nations of the world. One important point of balance to remember as you do ministry is that God called you to be different, not weird.

One last note about Noah's ark. There were probably hundreds of people who helped to build it, yet only eight were saved in it. Just because you are working for God does not automatically translate into you having a saving relationship with God. Remember Jesus' invitation for us *to be with Him*.

Effective prayer

Prayer—combined with action—changes situations, transforms individuals, restores cities, and brings back prodigals. If we take a look at the life of Nehemiah, we clearly detect a spirit of prayer and dependence on God in every aspect of his journey to restore the walls of Jerusalem. Note the following times that he prayed:

- When he heard bad news (Nehemiah 1:4)
- Before a life-changing meeting (Nehemiah 2:4, 5)
- When opposition arose (Nehemiah 6:8, 9)
- When something needed correction (Nehemiah 7:4, 5)
- When the people needed forgiveness (Nehemiah 9:1, 2)
- When he finished the book (Nehemiah 13:30, 31; notice the last line!)

We preach, teach, write, talk, and dream about prayer, yet few pray "without ceasing." The solution? Pray about it! Effective prayer has the following three basic characteristics:

1. It's specific. What are you praying about? James 5:13–15 advises that when you pray, be as specific as you can. Instead of saying, "God, please touch my neighbor's heart," pray something like this: "God, I would like my neighbor to start attending a Bible study I have in my house every week. Please allow me to have an opportunity to invite him this week." Notice the difference? One sounds nice, but it's too general. The other one is specific. My wife keeps a journal, and she prays specifically for people. When she asks, "What can I pray for?" she writes it down and intercedes. That is what I am talking about.

2. It's measurable. What result would you expect God to bring about? James 5:17, 18 tells us an effective prayer is one that you can pray in a way that you are able to measure the results. I pray that my kids go to church. I pray that their prayer lives improve. I pray that their taste for spiritual things is greater than the desire to sin.

3. It's constant. When should you pray about an issue or person (Colossians 1:9)? I have been praying for a sibling for more than five years. I have been praying for opportunities to enlarge my territory and reach a wider audience for ten years. I have seen some prayers answered right away, while some are taking longer. I can't control the outcome, but I can control whether I pray or not. My job and yours is to pray—so let's. Don't give up.

Let's remember

Before I finish this chapter, I want to leave with you three ideas:

1. Prayer can change situations, but it always *changes you.* Sometimes God changes the situation without involving you, but many times He uses praying people to change the circumstances around them. The moment you start praying, God starts transforming you from a thermometer into a thermostat.

2. Prayer precedes strategy, informs it, and helps it succeed. Prayer shows you what God is *already* doing in your city. The reason we pray is not to twist God's arm so He will give us what we want, but rather to connect us with Him so we can clearly see what His plan is.

3. Nothing happens until *you pray. Not much happens if you* only *pray.* Just as faith without works is dead, so is prayer without action. The action that immediately follows a prayer demonstrates the level of your faith. The last part of this book contains some resources you can use in your prayer action plan.

This is what I am praying for: "In visions of the night, representations passed before me of a great reformatory movement among God's people. Many were praising God. The sick were healed, and other miracles were wrought. A spirit of *intercession* was seen, even as was manifested before the great Day of Pentecost. Hundreds and thousands were seen visiting families and opening before them the word of God. Hearts were convicted by the power of the Holy Spirit, and a spirit of genuine conversion was manifest."[1]

What about you? Will you commit to pray and fast at least once a week this year for the prodigals in your community? God cares as much about those prodigals as you do. Let's join Him by connecting with Him.

May our goal every day be *to be with Him.*

RESPONSE

Kendall Turcios, lead pastor and church planter of Ignite Church in Miami, Florida

What do you think?

There is no question that prayer—*persevering prayer*—is the beginning, continuation, and ending of anything we do for reaching prodigals. The passage that comes to my mind most frequently is found in 1 Thessalonians 5:17: "Pray without ceasing" (NKJV). This kind of prayer never stops. The longer I live, the more I realize how desperately dependent I am and my need to be in prayer.

I am a Miami Dolphins football fan (cue the circus music please), and I recently read about Rob Konrad, a former fullback for the team. He was deep-sea fishing alone off the coast of West Palm Beach one day at about 1:00 P.M., when he hooked a fish just as a large wave hit, and it pulled him into the water. He wasn't wearing a life vest, and his boat kept going because it was on autopilot. He was nine miles out to sea. What were his options? He basically had two. He could drown or swim. He chose the latter. At 4:40 A.M. he reached the shore. I've been nine miles out to sea before. You can't even see land. This means that he began swimming toward the eastern shore without seeing it. He didn't quit. He persevered. He was stung many times by jellyfish, was circled by a shark, and he saw rescue helicopters pass by and not see him. This is a tremendous example of perseverance.

If prayer is to be effectual, it needs to be *persevering prayer;* not drive-by prayer but persevering prayer—a prayer that *never* stops!

Another passage that speaks compellingly to me about prayer is 2 Chronicles 7:14: "If My people who are called by My name will *humble* themselves, and pray and seek My face, and turn from their wicked ways, then I will hear from heaven, and will forgive their sin and heal their land" (NKJV; emphasis added).

I have to be honest with you; whenever I encounter that one church member who always seems to get on my nerves, who never seems to "get it" and seems to be completely out of sync with what we are trying to do, I know God put them there to get me to pray! I have to confess, if I had no pride, they wouldn't bother me.

This passage reveals that the number-one obstacle to prayer is pride. Every time I pray, I am acknowledging that I can't and God can. But in order to connect with the power in prayer, I must humbly admit that I need what God has.

What do you do?

In order to perseveringly pray for prodigals, you may need to reframe a lot of your thinking on prayer.

Prayer is not about eloquence. Many people struggle with

how to pray. They think that prayer is reciting cute and pretty words that sound nice so God will be moved and answer. I grew up in churches where people would get up and recite words in an awkward poetic form. I'm not sure where this originated, but if you ask anyone today how they relate to that, they may be more inclined to think Broadway. I visited a church this year that was still doing this. Why is this completely out of touch? you may be asking (or not). Because it doesn't seem genuine. It's rehearsed. It does not seem authentic. Jesus Himself exhorted His followers in this regard when He said, "And when you pray, do not use vain repetitions as the heathen do. For they think that they will be heard for their many words. Therefore do not be like them. For your Father knows the things you have need of before you ask Him" (Matthew 6:7, 8, NKJV).

Prayer only requires sincerity. Biblical, persevering prayer is real talk from you to God. It doesn't have to sound pretty, appropriate, or to your artificial definition of holy. Have you gone to churches where someone prays and uses words and vocal inflections that sound like they are trying to impress God? That doesn't impress me, but maybe there is someone in the congregation who is led to believe that this in fact is the way they need to pray. And because they've never used such elaborate words, or don't even know what they mean, it may hinder them from ever praying.

Prayer collaborates with what God is already doing. The good news about reaching prodigals is that God, through the presence of the Holy Spirit, is already with them. Some people may mistakenly believe that prodigals have been abandoned by God because they are not walking with Him. But the Bible says the exact opposite about prodigals. "Be strong and of good courage, do not fear nor be afraid. . . . [God] will not leave you nor forsake you" (Deuteronomy 31:6, NKJV). When you pray for prodigals, pray with the assurance that God is with them already. David continues reaffirming this biblical principle by singing,

> "Where can I go from Your Spirit?
> Or where can I flee from Your presence?
> If I ascend into heaven, You are there;
> If I make my bed in hell, behold, You are there"
> (Psalm 139:7, 8, NKJV).

Prodigals may even be in the pit of hell, but the Holy Spirit is with them, and our prayers for them collaborate with God in this. Biblically speaking, some prodigals may be in a more spiritually advantageous position than some people who are regularly attending church but are only playing church. Speaking of the church in Laodicea, Jesus says in Revelation 3:15, "I know your works, that you are neither cold nor hot. I could wish you were *cold* or hot" (NKJV; emphasis added). I'm sure Jesus would prefer hot over cold, but He does say cold is preferable to lukewarm. Remember this when praying for prodigals! They are better off spiritually than some church people.

The One-Hour Prayer Challenge

A compelling video on YouTube entitled "40 Million Minutes" says that the average person lives seventy-seven years and, among all their activities, they spend less than ten minutes a day in prayer. Another study I came across said that the Christians in America spend about two and a half minutes a day in prayer! I recently launched the One-Hour Prayer Challenge in my church. Forget doubling the national average to five minutes, let's do an hour!

My pastor friend Ruber Leal shared with me one strategy for praying for an hour: spend ten minutes on each letter of the acronym PRAISE.

P stands for *Praise.* Spend ten minutes praising and thanking God for what He's done.

R stands for *Repent.* Ask for forgiveness of your sins. If you're like me, you'll want more than ten minutes, but stick with ten anyway.

A stands for *Ask.* Ask for the things you want God to do for you personally.

I stands for *Intercession.* Lift up others and their needs. Pray for prodigals and the lost.

S stands for *Silence.* Spend ten minutes listening. Many times this makes people uncomfortable, but push through your discomfort and actually try to hear from God. Some people benefit from writing in a prayer journal at this time. Try writing a letter from God to yourself. You'll be surprised with the results.

E stands for *Expectancy.* Spend the last ten minutes claiming God's promises for your life and the lives of your loved ones.

Praying is a discipline. It takes time to learn to pray. But if we are to reach prodigals, it will take persevering prayer and becoming people of prayer.

Questions

1. How important are prayer, fasting, and worship in your church?

2. If prayer is so important for the restoration of the people of our cities, why is it ignored, dismissed, or neglected? What can you do personally to improve in this area? What specific principles can you learn from Nehemiah's experience that you can apply to your own city and circumstances?

3. After you pray for a neighbor, a community, or a problem in your city, what can you *do* about it? Be specific. Share some practical ideas on how you have put your faith into action this past week.

4. Think about your church board and committee meetings. How much time is spent seeking God's ideas and thoughts on a particular issue? How can you make prayer a priority in every meeting you have?

5. In what areas of your life are you waiting for circumstances to change instead of allowing God to use you to change the circumstances?

---

1. Ellen G. White, *Testimonies for the Church* (Mountain View, CA: Pacific Press®, 1948), 9:126; emphasis added.

6 ~ Love

Key idea: Need and not theology turned
the prodigal toward home.

*About the time his money ran out, a great famine swept over
the land, and he began to starve. He persuaded a local farmer to
hire him, and the man sent him into his fields to feed the pigs. The
young man became so hungry that even the pods he was feeding
the pigs looked good to him. But no one gave him anything.*

*When he finally came to his senses, he said to himself, "At home
even the hired servants have food enough to spare, and here I am
dying of hunger!"* —Luke 15:14–17, NLT

Have you ever wondered how Jesus, an unknown preacher
with an unpopular message, was so effective in reaching
crowds of people? It's a one-word answer: *love*. People did not
follow Jesus because of His diet. They were not attracted to
Him because of His dress. His compassion showed that you
can, at the same time, call people to holiness while loving
them intensely through the process.

In order to do that, you must love.

Prodigals don't care how much you know until they know
how much you care. Many times we have had a big mouth and
invisible arms in our communities. Part of the gospel proclamation is the discovery of the answers to the following three
questions:

- What are my community members' interests?
- What are their needs?
- What are their hurts?

I applied those principles in my last church. We went out into the community and asked people what their interests, needs, and hurts were. It was a simple survey, but very telling. It was interesting that only 30 percent of the people who lived in a five-block radius of the church knew who we were. That is pretty consistent with the percentage of people in the United States who are aware of us. When I hear people talking about persecution, I want to ask them: How are they going to persecute someone they don't even know exists?

From the survey we found the following results.

- Interests: children, marriage, health
- Needs: food, jobs, adequate medical coverage
- Hurts: abuse, abandonment, addictions

After conducting the survey, we developed programs to meet the needs. This transformed the church from a fortress-mentality, FUBU ("for us, by us") church to a community-oriented congregation. First of all, we were surprised that such a very small percentage of people we asked knew who we were. This made an impact on us, since it was a five-hundred-member church in the middle of the Hispanic community. Second, it helped us target our community more effectively.

Everywhere I go, I sense in our churches a dissatisfaction with the status quo and a desire to be more involved in our community. May God help us to develop and not destroy that desire.

It is interesting to see what need does inside a person. In the prodigal's life, it made him reevaluate his life and remember that he had a home and a father. There are needs all around us. Compassion is better shown than explained.

Is it biblical?

Sometimes as I am presenting this material, I get some pushback from people who say our job is to preach the gospel, not transform communities. Since our basis should be the Bible, let's look at some principles in Scripture and then some how-tos at the end of the chapter.

Jesus said . . .

"For even the Son of Man did not come to be served but to serve others and to give his life as a ransom for many" (Mark 10:45, NLT).

Many years ago, Ellen White stated:

Christ's method alone will give true success in reaching the people. The Saviour mingled with men as one who desired their good. He showed His sympathy for them, ministered to their needs, and won their confidence. Then He bade them, "Follow Me."

There is need of coming close to the people by personal effort. If less time were given to sermonizing, and more time were spent in personal ministry, greater results would be seen. The *poor* are to be relieved, the *sick* cared for, the *sorrowing* and the bereaved comforted, the *ignorant* instructed, the *inexperienced* counseled. We are to weep with those that weep, and rejoice with those that rejoice. Accompanied by the power of persuasion, the power of prayer, the power of the love of God, this work will not, cannot, be without fruit.[1]

Steve Sjogren, author of *Conspiracy of Kindness,* writes: "Small things done with great love will change the world." Jesus' method of reaching the cities where He ministered consisted of preaching and service, and so should ours: "How God anointed Jesus of Nazareth with the Holy Spirit and power, and *how he went around doing good* and healing all who were under the power of the devil, because God was with him" (Acts 10:38, NIV; emphasis added).

Notice the following text: "Or do you think lightly of the riches of His kindness and tolerance and patience, not knowing that the *kindness* of God leads you to repentance?" (Romans 2:4, NASB; emphasis added). Think for a moment about the implications of that passage.

- Fact: God's kindness leads to repentance. How is His kindness shown to people?
- Fact: God's kindness is expressed by the works of His people toward others!
- Fact: God's kindness, when expressed, causes others to praise God (see 2 Corinthians 9:13).

The takeaway from these passages is that our *earthly* kindness can have an *eternal* impact. When we serve, we are not just meeting needs, we are helping people to meet Him.

Principles and objectives

Service toward others has three underlying principles. As you prepare to touch your city with practical demonstrations of God's love, keep these in mind.

We serve because of Jesus. He is the reason we serve. He commanded it, modeled it, and blesses it (Ephesians 6:7).

We serve others. It's not about feeling good about ourselves. It's not about listing, publishing, or congratulating ourselves for being service oriented once a year. It's about meeting the needs of our communities with an "others-focused" spirit (Galatians 5:13).

We serve without expectations. Free means free. We look for opportunities to share God's love, but we serve with no strings attached, we take no donations, and we never charge (Matthew 6:2–4).

A service lifestyle accomplishes various objectives:

1. A service lifestyle is part of a divine expectation. It is helpful to understand that when we are standing before our Maker, He will not ask us to recite the eschatological timeline, but rather, "What did you do about My children who needed help?" (Matthew 25:34–36).

2. A service lifestyle takes us out of our comfort zone. It's more than outreach; it's reaching out, even to those who don't look, believe, speak, or act like us. That includes our enemies! (Matthew 5:46–48).

3. A service lifestyle breaks down barriers. It's all about love, and love can indeed "conquer all." When we express love, we break down preconceived concepts about the church and God. "Be devoted to one another in love. Honor one another above yourselves" (Romans 12:10, NIV).

It is wise to remember that there are *thirty-seven* recorded miracles of Jesus in the New Testament. There is *one* written sermon of Jesus (the Sermon on the Mount). This goes along with the counsel given: "If less time were given to sermonizing, and more time were spent in personal ministry, greater results would be seen."[2] The same book tells us to focus on four areas as we serve:

> The *poor* are to be relieved, the *sick* cared for, the *sorrowing* and the *bereaved* comforted, the *ignorant* instructed, the *inexperienced* counseled. We are to weep with those that weep, and rejoice with those that rejoice. Accompanied by the power of persuasion, the power of prayer, the power of the love of God, this work will not, cannot, be without fruit.[3]

Here is a helpful table for your strategy:

	Activity	Date to do	Date completed
People with financial needs			
People with health needs			
People with emotional needs			
People with educational needs			

Start here

If you want to be more effective in reaching your community, here are ten practical suggestions. Use them as a starting point, a checklist if you will.

1. Purpose. Start by checking your purpose. Is it clearly spelled out? Do you have an "elevator speech" in which you can articulate your community service vision in less than two minutes? At the end of the day, we serve because we love, not so we can be on the local news or give seminars to gloat about how much we serve.

2. Providers. Many organizations already provide services in your community. Instead of reinventing the wheel as we often do, why not join worthwhile organizations in what they are doing? Here is a good starting point: www.voa.org. Invite organizations whose purposes are akin to yours to the church. We need to be cautious about who we bring in, and what their agenda is, but we have to realize that we did not invent the wheel in most areas. Community and religious organizations have been doing at least some of what you are doing, usually for a longer period of time. In an event at one of my churches, we invited several organizations to participate, including a local Christian college counseling department and representatives from the local hospital and police department. Just their exposure to our church ministries opened many doors. Among other things, we received five hundred teddy bears, a grant for food, free cholesterol screening, and more than forty computers for a lab—all free of charge.

3. People. There are people in the community who do not belong to any organization but have a foundation or personal initiative that you can benefit from and help out in.

4. Partnerships. In every community there are usually industries that work for community enhancement. Making a visit and introducing your vision can foster goodwill and give you access to funds.

- Visit the local business association.
- Join the local ministerial alliance.
- Visit organizations like the Boys and Girls Clubs in your town.
- Visit your local food bank.

5. *Politicians.* Many times we have been reluctant to engage politicians, sometimes with good reason. One of the first things I do in a new pastoral job is to find and meet with the mayor, council members, and district representative. It's also not difficult to contact the governor and senator. Why should we connect with the powerful in our community?

- They can point us to areas of need.
- They can point us to other organizations.
- They can provide resources, volunteers, and funds.
  This can get tricky, so tread softly.

I usually introduce myself and tell the official that we have an interest in improving our community through a wholistic approach that includes physical, mental, emotional, and spiritual help. I ask them three questions:

- What are the greatest needs of this city?
- What organizations or people would you suggest I talk to?
- Are there any initiatives you are implementing that we should take a look at?

I have always found government officials ready to talk and willing to help. Even the most secular mayors welcome the constructive actions of Christians in the community.

6. *Survey.* The best people to tell you what the community needs are . . . are the people in the community! Use a very simple survey (see the appendix), or e-mail me for an electronic copy. Talk to the people who live around your church. Let their needs drive your action plan.

7. Sermons. Preach on service, study it in small groups, and speak about it in the board meetings. What gets highlighted gets approved and funded. Use your influence and your example to show the benefits of service so that it not only benefits the people we serve but also the people we serve with.

8. Subsidy. Actions validate vision. You can't really say community service is of high value to you when it has no budget and is relegated to a musty room with three senior citizens and a once-a-month feeding. It's interesting how funding follows vision (look at point number one again).

9. Sustained effort. One of the complaints of people in developing countries, and in the United States as well, is the phenomenon of Christians who show up, do some work, take a picture, and leave. Any type of significant involvement in the community must be a sustained involvement. That is why it's better to start small and steady than it is to try and join every organization and do every service project. Plan to start solid and continue for a long time.

10. Service. Don't plan endlessly. Don't try to get it perfect before you act. Don't wait till you have all the people, the funds, or the plans in place. Just start serving somewhere. Make it a way of life.

Final thoughts

Service broadens your impact. When we serve, we have an impact on three groups of people in a positive way: the ones who serve, the ones you serve, and the ones you serve with. This is especially important for the younger generation, who loves to see the church engaging the community in practical ways.

Service honors God, blesses people, and changes perceptions.

"Servant evangelism softens the hearts of persons who are not yet Christians—people who often think the church exists only for itself or that it only wants people's time and money. By doing a 'low-risk' activity that shows 'high grace,' those resistant to the faith may (now or in the future) become more open to the saving message of Jesus Christ."[4]

Service is more than an event. It is not something we do once in a while to placate the conscience, appease the leadership, or satisfy a requirement. In order to make this a priority in our churches, we must do the following four things:

- Schedule it
- Fund it
- Model it
- Speak about it

Are you ready to do this in your church? What activities and programs would have to be modified or even cut to make this a reality?

Remember that your actions must be accompanied by the power of God. "Accompanied by the power of persuasion, the power of prayer, the power of the love of God, this work will not, cannot, be without fruit."[5] Claim this text for yourself this week as you engage in a lifetime of service. Let's start a "servolution": "Serve wholeheartedly, as if you were serving the Lord, not people, because you know that the Lord will reward each one for whatever good they do, whether they are slave or free" (Ephesians 6:7, 8, NIV).

Before we conclude this chapter, I would like to address one more item, hoping that you will hear my heart on this. While it's true that our job is not to combat the societal ills at the expense of the gospel, making people into healthy sinners devoid of salvation, we do have a social responsibility that is as much a part of the gospel as understanding that God loves us. Ellen White, as she often does, puts it very eloquently:

> A religion that leads men to place a low estimate upon human beings, whom Christ has esteemed of such value as to give Himself for them; a religion that would lead us to be careless of human needs, sufferings, or rights, is a spurious religion. In slighting the claims of the poor, the suffering, and the sinful, we are proving ourselves traitors to Christ. It is because men take upon themselves the name of Christ, while in life they deny His character, that Christianity has so little power in the world. The name of the Lord is blasphemed because of these things.[6]

As I see it, there are three levels of community service:

- Charity—focuses on immediate need. The focus is today.
- Training—focuses on training for a better life. The focus is on tomorrow.
- Systems—focuses on changing laws, providing access, and leveling the playing field. The focus is on *always*.

Let me illustrate.

- Charity: we give a man a fish.
- Training: we teach a man to fish.
- Systems: we change the systems so that a man can own a lake to fish in.

Everyone Welcome

Following is another example.

- Charity: food bank
- Training: computer skills class
- Systems: first-time home owner

Here is one more example.

- Charity: temporary housing refuge for sex-trade slaves
- Training: retraining former sex slaves for good jobs
- Systems: working with legislators to enact tougher laws against sex-slave traders

My observation has been that many churches are mostly concentrating on charity, and sometimes training. Who is speaking truth to power? Who is engaging the powers that be on the systems level so that injustice is replaced by justice? How many of our leaders are seated at the table where systems decisions are made? I'm afraid that if we do not collaborate to influence change in the systems, we will continue the vicious cycle that keeps dysfunction as the fallback solution for many. Our greatest joy should come not from how many people we served but how many people we helped get to a place where they did not need to come for help anymore.

Eliminate the gospel from community service, and you end up with changed circumstances but unchanged hearts. Focus on a gospel presentation without meeting the needs of the community you serve (in all three ways), and you have people who understand theology on an empty stomach.

It's not just one or the other. It takes both. Always.

Let's love.

RESPONSE

Rebecca Davis, associate pastor at Berean Church in Atlanta, Georgia

What do you think?

Impact in the communities surrounding our churches is imperative but usually an afterthought. Impact and influence extend beyond our weekly community service initiatives and should be founded upon a goal that the community knows the church cares. However, the mentality of our churches has become so inwardly focused that unless reaching the community is done via traditional evangelism, there really is no additional thought given to the surrounding community. And the problem with this is that when we invite the people, they come. We don't really want them there. Everyone is not welcome! Our concerns extend no further than our own ministry departments. I also think that this becomes difficult for us because, even though our mentality is inward focused, we still inherently have no true sense of Christian community even within our own churches. Francis Schaeffer once said, "Our relationship with each other is the criterion the world uses to judge whether our message is truthful—Christian community is the final apologetic."[7]

People in the community know they can come to our churches for food distribution, for clothes, possibly even for help with an electricity bill, and they may even feel they can visit our churches from time to time. However, when they visit, there is no sense of community, love, and fellowship within our own building, much less beyond the four walls.

I think it's imperative to begin at the place where we create the culture within our churches of love. This must be a focus of the pastor, which he pours into his leaders, who in turn pour into the membership at large. I believe then we will begin to understand the importance of extending our "community" beyond ourselves. It will spill over into the surrounding neighborhoods.

Following this, I recommend the ten practical steps in this chapter as an excellent checklist for service in the community: Purpose, Providers, People, Partnerships, Politicians, Survey, Sermons, Subsidy, Sustained Effort, and Service. Service must be the culture of the church born out of love which leads to an individual, as well as a collective, burden to reach others. The burden of love and service must be a shared burden so that the responsibility is felt among the entire church, and everyone recognizes the importance of funding service and partnering with the community.

What do you do?

I have had the opportunity to create a wholistic young adult ministry called Connect, which includes worship services, small groups, social activities, and outreach. The outreach ministry is called Together Achieving Greatness (TAG). Our motto is "TAG, you're it!" The concept behind TAG is that we focus on random acts of kindness in the community, because being relevant is our primary goal. The "acts" involve cosmetic improvements and positive events within the surrounding neighborhoods. We go into the community expecting absolutely nothing in return. We are not looking for the community to come to our services, and we are not expecting them to give us a huge thank you. We perform random acts of kindness simply to let the community know we are here and we care. Our goal was that eventually this would lead to partnerships with other churches and community groups to affect real change in the community. Since TAG's inception, we have partnered with local charities such as The Love and Give Foundation, and we are currently partnering with the National Center for Civil and Human Rights to help fight against human trafficking.

The first TAG initiative was done by my Connect leadership team. We wanted to make sure the culture began with us. We went to the local gas station and helped pay for gas. We literally saw the concept of "pay it forward" unfold before our eyes. A young man that we "TAG-ed" said to us, "You guys have blessed me. Now I am going to go and bless someone else." After this we knew that we had to get our young adult constituents excited about service and outreach. We began a competition of sorts among our young adults to see who could come up with the best TAG. The young adults created teams that went out into the community of their choice and TAG-ed people using their respective kindness ideas. They were to document by recording video with their phones or cameras, to be shown at a Connect worship service. It was an amazing endeavor in that we actually had a couple donate a car and TAG a family with it (of course, you know this couple won the contest!). One of our Connect franchises recently went out in their community because the Super Bowl was being held there, and they TAG-ed people who answered questions about football and the Bible.

TAG-ing someone might include handing them a ticket or card that has "TAG, you're it" printed on it. The card has our name, address, and service times on it. Although we pray they will visit our Facebook page, come to our services, or whatever, we do not assume that they will ever contact us. That's not our motivation. However, when TAG-ed, you are now "it" to TAG someone else in the community. And while our budget is low, we believe so much in this ministry that oftentimes we have funded TAG out of our own pockets. Not doing TAG is not an option for us.

TAG has reinforced in our minds and in our ministry that outreach to our communities cannot be an afterthought. Thus, we uplift TAG just as much as our worship service. All franchises have to agree from the onset to implement, sometimes even before starting a worship service, the TAG ministry. It's in our Connect DNA to serve, and it has opened doors to partnerships and trust in the community.

Questions

1. If Jesus lived in your community, what do you think He would spend His days doing? Be specific . . . dream a little.

2. How do we stay consistent with the "service with no strings attached" principle and, at the same time, look for opportunities to share Jesus with the people we are serving? Where is the balance between not pressuring people and yet being aware of "God moments" we can use to share our faith?

3. How can you involve the youth in your church in these projects?

4. What is the reason why most churches are not service oriented?

5. If you were starting a church from scratch, how would you weave this principle into the life of the new church?

1. Ellen G. White, *The Ministry of Healing* (Mountain View, CA: Pacific Press®, 1905), 143, 144; emphasis added.

2. Ibid., 143.

3. Ibid., 143, 144; emphasis added.

4. "Servant Evangelism," Northside Christian Church, accessed November 23, 2015, http://www.northsidecc.org/#/outreach/servant-evangelism.

5. White, *The Ministry of Healing*, 144.

6. Ellen G. White, *Thoughts From the Mount of Blessing* (Mountain View, CA: Pacific Press®, 1956), 137.

7. Francis A. Schaeffer, *The Church at the End of the 20th Century* (Downers Grove, IL: InterVarsity, 1977), 137.

7 ~ Act

Not long after that, the younger son got together all he had, set off for a distant country and there squandered his wealth in wild living.　　　　　　　　　　　　　*—Luke 15:13, NIV*

When my son was younger, he was riding in the car with me on our way home one day. He asked me a simple question, the type of question that kids ask their dads. I replied by telling him: "Jonathan, remind me when we get home to show you a text from Daniel that will answer that question."

My son looked at me and said, "Dad, who is Daniel, and why did he send you a text?"

This interaction articulates part of the challenge of connecting with the next generation. They hear us; they just don't understand us.

Ministry to young people has always been of interest to me. Then I had teenagers, which took that interest to a whole new level. I believe that outside of death, one of the worst things that could happen to me is to see my children decide to leave the faith. Since I want my kids in heaven, I want to do everything I can to show them Jesus instead of the exit sign.

We have been dealing with God's plan for the church. Although it has been damaged, it is not beyond repair. Many distractions keep us from fulfilling our mission: infighting, politics, apostasy, extremism, apathy, sin, power plays. In some churches, it is easier to add a fourth person to the Trinity than it is to change the color of the paint in the foyer. In our effort to be different, we sometimes have become weird and, worse yet, irrelevant. In some communities, if the Adventist church were to disappear tomorrow, would it be missed? The answer is often no.

One particular segment of the population that is especially disconnecting from the church is millennials. At the time of this book being published, they are roughly from sixteen to twenty-eight years of age. My heart breaks for the more than one thousand churches in the North American Division (NAD) that do not have a single millennial attending. These young people don't fight. They just leave.

While we are fighting among ourselves, with our FUBU (for us, by us) brand of Christianity, the world around us is rapidly changing. Two books I would like to refer you to point out some very disturbing trends: *unChristian: What a New Generation Really Thinks About Christianity . . . and Why It Matters* and *You Lost Me: Why Young Christians Are Leaving Church . . . and Rethinking Faith*. Both published by Baker Books for the Barna Group, these studies bring to light some troubling perceptions of Christianity in America. While these studies analyzed Christianity in general, the results should be looked at very carefully because they could very well apply to the church we all love.

Disturbing findings

The first disturbing trend is that the younger generation, up to about age twenty-nine, has more agnostics in it than any previous generation. In other words, the younger they are, the less they believe. In fact, the percentage of people who describe themselves as having no religion doubled in the past ten years. Couple that with the Adventist Church growing at 3 percent a year, and it's easy to see we have a problem, especially with the younger generation.

The following percentages are worrisome and should be a wake-up call.

Generation	Age	Percentage of agnostics	Number in U.S.A.
Mosaic & Busters	18–41	37%	34 million
Mosaic & Busters	16–29	40%	24 million
Boomers	42–60	27%	21 million
Elders	61+	23%	12 million

In North America, even though thousands of committed young Adventists live out their faith every day, the average age in an Adventist congregation is close to sixty and getting older. As I travel the country, I get to meet many people of different cultures, but I am more familiar with Hispanic Adventism. In most Hispanic churches, the membership is young, younger, and youngest. This would tell me that the average age in an English-speaking church might be even higher than the statistics say. Somewhere along the way, we stopped being as effective in reaching the younger generation with an unchanging message. Some believe that just putting in a drum set and singing a couple of praise songs will produce the "it" factor. Others feel that we have to return to the "old ways." How we become relevant, authentic, and life-changing to this generation and the next remains a baffling mystery to many congregations. While I believe that inspiring worship is a must, worship is more than just what you do one hour a week in a building. We are called not to just hold on to what we have but to reach more people every day with this last-day, special message.

A close family member of mine, who is in his early seventies, has a passion and desire to see Cuba freed from communism. When he was a young soldier more than forty years ago, he was hours from getting on a plane and parachuting into Cuba to support the Bay of Pigs invasion, which failed miserably. Since that time, a group of hundreds, maybe thousands of Cuban resistance fighters has trained regularly in the humid swamps of South Florida, waiting for the day that the invasion finally happens and Cuba is free again. There is only one problem. There has been a lot of training, more than forty years' worth of it, but no actual combat. It's kind of funny (although I won't tell him) to see them getting together every year to talk about their plan, have strategy sessions, and share the latest news about the war that no one is fighting.

Most are retired now, but to hear them speak, you would think that they are ready to take on the Cuban army right now. I am sure the Castro brothers wet their pants at night thinking about the (ever-decreasing) number of commandos who will, with their canes and hearing aids, descend into Cuba and annoy the communist government by leaving their turn signals on. This last summer, this same family member received a lifetime award. That's right. A lifetime award. For what? He has never fired a single bullet!

I am afraid that the scene is all too familiar. Not to discredit the older generation, for we are all heading that way, and they, too, have an important job to do, but what happens when they go to their sleep? Who will finance the church? Is the younger generation ready to step up in commitment to God's remnant church? Are we empowering the younger generation to take over, or are we so caught up in ourselves that we neglect to elect and deploy the "army of youth"?

Our largest mission field is North America!

Another trend is the way millennials perceive Christians to be. You might ask, Why should we care about what lost people think? Aren't they lost anyway? Hasn't Satan clouded their minds to such a point that nothing they have to say is worth listening to? If we look at Jesus' example, we see that He took into consideration the needs, opinions, and perceptions of the people that He wanted to minister to. Perceptions matter. If the pre-Adventists are going to jump ranks and join the *good side,* we need to start where they are, not where we are.

A sobering statistic jumps out at us in the attitudes toward different types of Christians among sixteen- to twenty-nine-year-olds. The table below shows attitudes toward Christians in general, evangelical Christians, and born-again Christians:

Impression	Christian	Evangelical	Born Again
Bad impression	38%	49%	35%
Neutral	45%	48%	55%
Good impression	16%	3%	10%

And among the specific views of millennials about the way Christians think, ponder this: non-Christians perceive us to be

1. anti-homosexual (91 percent);
2. judgmental (87 percent);
3. hypocritical (85 percent); and
4. out of touch (72 percent).

Only a small percentage believed that the following characteristics are the ones that best describe Christians: *respect, love, hope, trust, genuine,* and *real.*

What these statistics tell us is the need for the church to be incarnational—to get its hands dirty while keeping a clean heart—and to show by its actions what one thousand slogans won't accomplish. It's impossible to give the answers when we don't even know the questions!

This is not just numbers and stats to me. A very close family member let me know a while back that he is choosing to be an agnostic. This is someone who grew up in the church, in a pastoral family, but has rejected the faith of his youth. As I wrote this chapter, I prayed for him. It's my desire to see him in heaven, and I struggle to find answers to some of his questions. Since I can't believe for him, I have to trust that the Holy Spirit will do His work in his life, and that I will do my part so that when he does decide to give faith another try, we will have the type of church God wants us to have.

Once, when I was sharing the material found in this chapter with pastors in a meeting, one of the men present stood up and told me that if he had a conversation with my relative, he could "fix" him in a half hour. That illustrates the point I am trying to make. This man was so out of touch with reality that he presumed he could answer the questions people are not asking.

If you would like to pray for my relative, I would really

appreciate it. Most of us have a daughter, brother, or close friend in the same situation, and if you would like for our family to pray for that person, e-mail me and I will pray for them.

Points of disconnection

There are six points of disconnection for millennials. Please don't kill the messenger! Don't dismiss the study offhand, or blame them, or yourself, or culture. Instead, *act*. Do something! Following are the six points:

1. *Overprotective.* Millennials feel they have helicopter parents. They perceive church as demonizing everything that does not have the "Christian" label, afraid of the world, and creating a false separation. The church does not want to deal with complex issues. I've said it before, when Jesus is not the center, there is a vacuum that fills up with personal preferences and pet peeves, not biblical principles.

2. *Shallow.* They see a church that has no connection to real life. They see church with a slogan similar to Vegas: "What happens in church stays in church." Forty-seven percent of millennials have no deep connection with a member in church. There's no real opportunity to lead. That is why service is so important to this generation.

3. *Antiscience.* They see church members as thinking that reason and faith are enemies and science and religion are incompatible. The church is not willing to address the tough questions.

4. *Repressive* in the area of sexuality. Since the church has many times been quiet or just said no without any thorough discussion, the surrounding culture is determining many of their beliefs. We must not be afraid to address

tough questions and have difficult conversations on
sexuality.

5. *Doubtless.* They did not find the church to be a place
where questions were valued. But doubt is "the ants in
the pants of faith" (Frederick Buechner). The worst possible type of doubt, the most insidious and damaging, is
unexpressed doubt. If churches are not safe places to ask
questions, then where? With whom?

6. *Exclusive.* They found the church more interested in
building walls to keep to its own, than bridges, and not
friendly to outsiders. They also had difficulty finding
churches where there was no racial majority.

Millennials in Adventist churches in North America scored
higher in the same survey (see the table[1] below). In this case,
higher is not better (think golf, not football).

Christian Millennials		
Doubtless	• U.S. 10%	SDA 28%
Exclusive	• U.S. 22%	SDA 34%
Anti-science	• U.S. 25%	SDA 47%
Overprotective	• U.S. 23%	SDA 36%
Shallow	• U.S. 24%	SDA 29%
Repressive	• U.S. 25%	SDA 37%

CLINT JENKIN PHD | barna.org

Barna Group

Seven practical solutions

Here are some action steps you can take:

1. Change your vision of the purpose of church. The church doesn't exist to *prepare* the next generation. It is a *partnership* of generations that are fulfilling God's purposes in this end time. Think about it. When you need help with your DVD player, who do you call, little Johnny or Grandpa? David Kinnaman calls this "reverse mentoring."[2] We don't know it all; in fact, we can learn a great deal from the new generation.

2. Be intentional about connecting job and faith. Adventist education is essential in this area. Most of the millennials who disconnected from church said they never saw the connection between what they did for a living and their faith. God does not call only pastors. He calls carpenters and housekeepers and CEOs. That connection is invaluable. Preach and teach that on a regular basis.

3. Give them real power—boards, elders—real leadership. I've looked through the Bible and have yet to find anyone serving as a "junior deacon." In a church where I spoke, the board of elders had been the same for twenty years. No one else was good enough to be promoted, it seemed. If you are a leader reading this, please consider appointing to leadership positions people who are in the millennial generation. I made it a point to appoint youth to nominating committees. At first, people were resistant because of the drama that usually happens. After several years, those young people are now leaders.

4. Stand in the gap. Protect them. Give them permission

to fail. I have already decided to be an Adventist. No matter what happens, I'm staying. Many teenagers and young adults are still in the process of deciding. Keep them away from the self-appointed Elijahs in your church. Don't go for what is politically advantageous but what is right. If you are going to err, err on the side of loving too much.

5. Strive for deep, long-lasting relationships. What if every young person had a mentor? What if that mentor could show them what grace is like, what it means to walk with God? What if the mentor could be available for counsel and prayer?

6. Turn doubt into doing through opportunities for service. It's my personal belief that every young person should have at least one opportunity to go on a mission trip. It transforms lives.

7. Listen. Then guide. They have a cacophony of voices talking to them but no one who listens to them. You be that one.

Final thoughts

Let's empower the next generation. If we keep saying they are the church of tomorrow, there will be no church tomorrow! Change will come when the pain of losing our children is greater than the desire to do things the same way we have always done them.

1. We need spiritual, gifted young people in key positions of influence. The devil can't have all the good jobs!

2. We need to understand that God speaks to young people too. Do you believe this? Do your actions reflect that fact?

3. We need to value, appreciate, and encourage men and

women who are bold enough to finish God's work.

As I mentioned earlier, I have a close family member who is far from God. I am hoping that when he decides to come back to church, that the day he shows up, these things happen:

- The person who greets him is happy my brother is there, and he is happy also.
- The young adults in that church will sit next to him and engage him in conversation.
- Someone will invite him to lunch.
- The message is inspiring, dealing with real-life issues that seek to transform, not impress.
- The music is well done and singable.
- They will keep him away from the member who was baptized in vinegar.
- Someone will learn his name and look him in the eye.

In essence, what I am praying for is that people at the church will wake up that Sabbath morning knowing that a prodigal might show up and act accordingly.

Now, how about you? How about your church? What will you do? How will you act?

RESPONSE

Dave Ketelsen, lead pastor of Hamilton Community Church in Chattanooga, Tennessee

What do you think?

First of all, I think a book like this is long overdue, especially in Adventism. I appreciate your boldness in addressing such a difficult and pushed-off subject.

How you begin this chapter is absolutely brilliant. I love a challenge. When you and your son Jonathan were on completely different pages, it revealed how far apart we are from where we need to be in connecting with this millennial generation.

When you pointed out how this generation of young people won't fight, they'll just leave, that also broke my heart. I thought of how many have already left and if we'll ever get them back. They're in my prayers so often.

I think your findings are disturbing and maddening as you point out how we've nearly lost this generation. But the cold hard facts are before us, and I think we not only need to pay attention, we need to act.

What really hit me in this chapter was your statement, *"It's impossible to give the answers when we don't even know the questions."* That statement has haunted me. You're absolutely right, we're not connecting, and when they do hear us, they don't understand us. We're on completely different planets.

When you mentioned how these numbers and stats go beyond that to a very close family member (I immediately said a prayer for him) and how this well-intentioned dragon stood up and said he could fix him in a half hour, my, how I wanted to sit down with this man for half a day . . . and then maybe not.

The story you tell of how your family member trained so hard to free Cuba and nothing has ever happened made me think of how often we talk about how we want to use our young people, but if we're not using them, talk is not only cheap, it's also destructive.

When we do involve them, we often criticize them or want

to take back the reins. I've seen it happen over and over. The older generation verbalizes a need for youth to be active in the church, but when the youth do something, it's usually not what the older generation wants. So they feel they have to stay in control and be the gatekeepers.

I think it would be good for them to go back to when they were young and how they viewed church. Many would have loved the opportunity to have made some changes and see more life in the church.

I like the personal touch you provide your readers in the way they can e-mail you and you will pray for their son, daughter, or close friend. That made an impression on me. This book is not about information, it's about transformation.

I appreciate your focus on keeping before our church its mission and purpose; otherwise, we'll never use the next generation. They need to be empowered in real leadership positions. I think that's imperative if you're going to see this Advent movement move.

Asking for a response and questions at the end of the chapter helped me to reflect on what I just read. It also motivated me to see what I'm doing in my church to involve and keep our youth engaged. I've been motivated to do a better job in developing ministry opportunities for our youth.

I also love how you encourage your readers to listen to them. In order to listen, we have to be silent and really hear them out. (*Silent* and *listen* have the same letters.) *Our early pioneers were a bunch of teenagers!*

I look around me, and I want to go and choke about twenty pastors right now (in a Christian kind of way) and say, "Wake up! We're losing our young people while you're arguing over _____." (Fill in the blank.) That's what I think!

What do you do?

1. First we need to ask ourselves, "Do we really want all young people in our churches? Or do we actually mean that we want to preserve our values in a younger generation that is a prototypical image of ourselves? And are we willing to make the gospel compelling enough by trying to actually live it?"

Recently I went to our youth department and asked our young people what they like about their church and if there were some things they would like to see happen. I also asked them what they would like to hear their pastor preach about. Their answers were helpful, and their teachers told me what an impression it made on their generation to feel like they had a voice and influence in their church.

The young people were telling me, and the church's leadership, "I'm not just looking to attend church; I want to actually give something." Many of the young people I interviewed did want to give something back. This is a generation that has been raised on the ethic of service. Many have been doing volunteer work since grade school or earlier.

Seeing our youth and young people involved and up front attracts other young people.

2. You could get the sense, if you're a millennial walking through the door of many churches, that you could come and go and no one would really miss you. So we are intentionally making sure our greeters connect with this generation and make them feel so good about coming to church that they not only want to come back but that they also want to bring their friends. We provide opportunities for them to connect with other young people and get involved in service activities and small groups.

3. Our nominating committee has intentionally invited

our young people to serve in leadership positions (not junior positions). They know their voice is respected and heard in our Leadership Team Meetings (board meetings). They know they have the freedom to fail and fall. They're valued and have much to contribute. Not only are they capable young people, but often they may have more time and flexibility than the thirty- or fifty-somethings who are juggling careers and children. Include your young people in church so that they are not merely spectators of adults doing church but are full participants.

There are seven words that will ruin any church. "We have always done it this way!" Allowing our youth to make some of these changes and have a voice in that process is healthy for them and us.

I think our young people need to be able to serve with people who are older than them so that mature Christians with experience can partner with them. (*We'll keep them away from the member who was baptized in vinegar.*) On the flip side, older people need younger people to serve with so they can be reminded of the vigor and enthusiastic potential of youth. Added to this is the display of God's wisdom and glory to the world when such a diverse group of people come together because of their unity in Christ.

Churches are not perfect—nor should we ever think they will be—but as long as church people do mean things to people who are a little different, we shouldn't be surprised when *no* young people want to attend these churches.

4. "You don't get to reach who you want, you reach who you are." If we're really all about youth, then we will be a church using our youth. Keep them involved in what they enjoy doing! Have them fill out a survey in which they share what their spiritual gifts are, and ask them to help lead out

with music, greeting, and other functions. The other benefit of young people setting down roots in a multiage, inclusive church service is that they're more likely to stay on in church past their teenage years.

We can never just talk about missions and expect our young people to understand. Young people need to experience mission firsthand; and it doesn't have to be a short-term trip to a foreign country. Organizing local outreaches with our teens could be as simple as painting a widow's house, working at a rescue mission, or visiting a rest home. At my church we feed the homeless every Sunday at 3:00 P.M.

If a young person has only been involved in age-specific ministries and not included in serving in a multiage church, then it's typical at that point that many young people stop going to church. But if a young person has always been involved in serving in a multiage church, when they reach the end of high school they have the benefit of a community that hasn't shifted with each passing age-group, and a place where they have stability.

One of the most difficult areas of ministry for many churches is in the area of delegation. The "I will do it all" mentality might be great for the smoothness of the program, but it can be horrible for growth in the lives of your youth. You can always look for ways to train and equip your young people.

When it comes to delegating, Dave Stone's "Four Phases of Ease" are really helpful:

1. I do it, and you watch.
2. I do it, and you do it.
3. You do it, and I watch/assist.
4. You do it, and I'll do something else.

Act

Jesus called young people to be His disciples. As we enable and equip servanthood in our youth, they will find the joy of serving, and this will encourage them to stay committed to the church they grew up in.

Questions

1. What would a mentorship program look like in your church? Who are you mentoring?
2. How can we be "cutting edge" without "cutting corners"? How can we connect without compromising?
3. Of the five disconnection challenges, which one does your church struggle with the most? What practical steps can you take to change that reality?
4. What *one* thing are you motivated and dedicated to do in order to engage, reclaim, and develop young adults in your church?

---

1. Slide drawn from Clint Jenkin, "Seventh-day Adventist Millennials: Up or Out?" Barna Group, North American Division Conference, November 2013, accessed November 23, 2015, https://www.adventistarchives.org/toward-a-coherent-knowledge-base-on-church-retention-and-engagement.pdf.

2. David Kinnaman, *You Lost Me: Why Young Christians Are Leaving Church . . . and Rethinking Faith* (Grand Rapids, MI: Baker Books, 2011), 12.

8 ~ New

Key idea: One of the best ways of connecting with
"far-off" people is to plant a church.

*So he returned home to his father. And while he was still a long
way off, his father saw him coming. Filled with love and compassion, he ran to his son, embraced him, and kissed him.*

—Luke 15:20, NLT

I arrived at 10:30 A.M., right when breakfast and Bible classes
around tables usually start. After a healthy breakfast, we went
to the sanctuary, where the worship service was intentional
and to the point. Music, prayer, and the message followed by
tithes and offerings and a short announcement. We were eating another healthy potluck by 12:15 P.M.

Triad Adventist Church is a church plant in North Carolina.
One of the best ways to provide prodigals a way to reconnect
is planting churches that are ready when they come back and
happy that they are there. I want you to prayerfully consider
whether God is calling you to plant a church that prodigals can
come back to. To be absolutely transparent with you, I have
found it much harder to improve an established church than to
start a new one with prodigal-welcoming DNA embedded in it.

In Triad, I was reminded of three ways that church plants
make a difference:

1. "I fit here." More than one person I spoke to that morning expressed the same sentiment: "This church has given me an opportunity to use my talents." That is a consistent occurrence in church plants. People who were relegated to pew warming suddenly find themselves leading and serving. No matter the intentionality of the mother church, there are only so many offices to be filled. New churches provide new opportunities and levels of involvement. And one more significant item: this church plant is *lay led*. It's growing. It is making an impact. Without paid clergy. Imagine that.

2. *"I came back here."* Several families, young adults, and even former church leaders who had stopped attending have returned. It's amazing what having a grace orientation does for a church. The focus I saw in Triad is a greater preoccupation with serving and reaching the community than for the myriad of secondary issues we often divide over. As one of the members put it: "I've been waiting for this church for fifty-eight years." New churches provide an option for people who have been burned, bypassed, or bored.

3. *"I love it here."* In previous chapters we realized the obvious fact that Adventist churches have a challenge retaining their youth. As I looked into the Triad audience that morning, I could see a cross section of people represented.

- Different age-groups: This was not a "youth church." It was a church with a little of everyone.
- Different backgrounds: former Adventists, new members, nonmembers, longtime members.
- Different races: It was diverse, and that is a great thing.

The most important question I left with after visiting Triad was this: Where are the other church plants? If it's proven statistically that one of the best (maybe *the* best) ways of doing evangelism is planting a church, where are all the new churches being planted? Where is the strategy for new churches in each city?

Reality check

A while back I had the chance to sit down with several young adults and listen to their thoughts on the church. It was a very candid conversation. Some were faithful in attendance, while others were not. Some had rejected the church of their youth altogether. All wanted to talk. From the conversation, one clear thought became evident, especially from the ones who still attended church: We are interested in participating— not being spectators.

Another conversation with a young adult who had left the church more than ten years earlier led him to ask me a pointed question: "Do you have young people in place in management positions at all levels of the church?"

I answered truthfully (and painfully) that we did not, and then thought to myself, *Why don't we?* Maybe the reason is that we have equated youth with inexperience and think that age translates into effectiveness. The truth is that your age doesn't automatically mean you're able or mature or effective. Talent is ageless. Take, for example, the thirty-four-year-old CEO of Burger King, a multibillion-dollar company where stake-holders old enough to be his grandparents entrust millions of dollars to this young kid.[1] You mean to tell me that our church has no one like that?

Their frustrations are real: frustration about inflexibility; frustration about majoring in minors; frustration about red tape even at the local church level. Frustration pushed some of them to join other local Adventist churches or to leave the church or to become passive members in the church they attend or, for a select few, to start a brand-new church. The question is, What outlets are in place in your congregation to deal with the frustration that young members feel? They don't need your pity or condescension; they need your attention. They need you to listen. It is hard to avoid being defensive and to bite your tongue instead. I believe that one of our problems is that we have not taken the time to listen to this invisible generation. We talk too much. Young people have information overload, but no one who really listens to them. I invite you to set up appointments and events with the express intention of listening. Listen first, then guide.

As I said before, sometimes it's easier to plant a new church than it is to improve an existing one. New churches, although not necessarily for youth, can be points of attraction to a generation of millennials that has the highest percentage of unchurched people in the history of this country.

What do we do?

We start new churches! This, to me, is the most successful way of reaching prodigals. There are several new churches in the NAD. Here is a sampling of those that began before this book was published, although this is not an exhaustive list by any means:

Mosaic (www.mosaicadventist.com)
Journey (www.comejourney.org)
Impact (www.facebook.com/impactsdachurch)
Resurrection (www.resurrectionsda.org)
Lifespring (lifespringadventist.org)
Arise (www.arisesda.com)

Zion (www.facebook.com/ZionSDA)
Epic (www.epicwiredsda.com)
Ignite (www.myignitechurch.org)
Remix (www.remixadventist.com)
Triad (www.triadadventistfellowship.org)

Two characteristics are common to all of these churches:

1. They minister to a younger (although not exclusively), multicultural crowd.
2. They were not in existence fifteen years ago. None of them. Most of them were not even ten years old at the time of this writing.

Expectations

If you plant a church that reaches all but is intentional in welcoming millennials, you can expect the following:

- *Expect resistance.* I have not encountered many new churches (or any church plants for that matter) that have been started with complete acceptance. I have planted six myself, and I have never experienced total support from either the mother church or neighboring congregations. It's safe to say that not only are they opposed, but they experience a higher level of opposition from church members who are concerned about music, about their own youth leaving, and have the "Why do we need another church?" rationale, among other objections. Expect resistance, but it's worth it.
- *Expect lack of commitment.* It's naïve to expect a generation that has been told for so many years to stay

on the sidelines to all of a sudden understand what it takes to play the game. In most of these churches, it takes years to develop leaders. Don't get frustrated by the lack of buy-in. Continue to train and empower. It's worth it.

- *Expect slower growth than ethnic churches.* Ethnic churches usually experience rapid growth. This does not happen much in the native culture, and you should not feel bad because you aren't baptizing a hundred every year like the Spanish or Haitian church down the street. I have been tracking new churches for more than fifteen years and have not seen one explode with thousands joining it in the first five years. That is not to say that they are not out there, but I have not seen them. Yet, most of them have grown, stabilized, and are winning their peers who count themselves in some of the least-reached demographics in North America. Keep looking for ways to do evangelism. It's worth it.

- *Expect mistrust.* It takes time to gain millennials' trust. Many of them have been hurt or neglected by the church of their parents, if they ever had a church at all. Millennials have unprecedented access to information, and they often believe they are as much of an expert as any adult in a particular topic. You don't automatically get their trust; you must earn it by having patience, developing deep relationships, and by backing up what you say. Once you get their trust, it's worth it.

- *Expect conversions.* Most of the churches I have been tracking have experienced real conversions of nonchurched people—not just biological or transfer growth. Seeing someone come to faith in Jesus is an experience like no other. It's worth it.

Why not

Hopefully you or someone close to you will get the vision to plant churches to reach prodigals. There are a million reasons why, but before you start, here are five reasons why not. Let's plant churches for the right reasons:

1. You want to "show them" at [insert denominational institution, church, or person's name here] *how it's really supposed to be done.* You have an axe to grind or a wrong to be avenged. This is starting a church for what you are against instead of what you are for. We should carry a *cross* on our shoulders, not a chip.

2. You just want to be the boss. You want to be in charge and do things your way. No longer the associate, you are now "the man" or "the woman." It will be great to remember who you are: you are neither "the man" nor "the messiah" nor "the manager." You are a servant leader, in that order. The fastest path to failure is the inability to admit you don't know everything. One thing you will quickly realize is that being "the man" is not as glamorous as it seems!

3. You think it would be "nice to try this." This is a great reason for opening a new restaurant—but not so much for a new church. Many have tried church planting before. There are resources available to do it right; be sure and get them. There are proven methods in place to help you; use them. Before you jump in with both feet, make sure you are jumping in the right pool. Prodigals don't need another person who starts and then quits on them.

4. Your spiritual life has been down for a while. Maybe this seems like the adventure you need. But remember, church planting is not a spiritual remedy. It will take everything you have, and then more, to see it through. Sometimes when things have been stale for us, we think a change of scenery is exactly what we need. Maybe the change needs to happen inside first, instead of letting your surroundings determine your spirituality.

5. Your personal/family life is strained at the moment. Church planting increases stress. Its highs are usually higher, and its lows are usually lower. A strong family unit of your own will help you through those hard times that are sure to come. Invest time in strengthening your core family group.

Move ahead

Now that you have eliminated the reasons for not planting, you are ready to plant. According to David T. Olson, there are ten good reasons to plant a church.[2] Here are the top ones:

1. New churches lower the age profile of the American church, increase its multi-ethnicity, and better position the whole church for future changes.

2. New churches provide synergistic benefits to established churches. Research shows that denominations that plant many strong churches have healthier, growing, established churches than those who plant few churches.

3. New churches provide a channel to express the energy and ideas of passionate, innovative young pastors. Church planting encourages the development of the gifts of ministry and leadership. Denominations that plant few churches unintentionally focus on training pastors in stabilizing gifts. A denomination needs both stabilizing and expansionist gifts to

be both healthy and growing.

4. New churches are the research and development unit of God's kingdom. New churches create most of the current models and visions for healthy life. Healthy cultural adaptations and theological vitality occur more often in a denomination that excels at church planting, because the ferment of new ideas and ministry solutions is more robust.

5. New churches are historically the best method for reaching each new generation. While many established churches have the ability to connect with the younger cohort, each generation also seems to need their own new types of churches that speak the gospel with their own cultural values and communication style.

6. New churches are more effective than established churches at conversion growth. Studies show that new churches have three to four times the conversion rate per attendee than established churches.

7. Because the large majority of Americans do not attend a local church, many more new churches are needed. In 2005, 17.5 percent of Americans attended a local church. Seventy-seven percent of Americans do not have a consistent connection with a Christian church.

Now, having taken stock of what you have read, understanding the need and the reality of this generation, what are you going to do about it? Will you prayerfully consider planting or joining a church plant?

In 2007, I was pastoring a church in the Pacific Northwest. God had blessed us with growth, and we had three services and three pastors. We got to the point where we needed to either move and build a bigger, better facility or plant a new church.

We planted. We started a multicultural church that now has more than one hundred in attendance. We started another Hispanic church nearby that has more than 250 members. That same church had planted another congregation around five years earlier. Where there had been one church ten years earlier, there were now four. We multiplied the kingdom impact instead of just growing by addition.

I remember finding a letter from long ago in my desk one day. In it, a concerned leader bemoaned the fact that a church was being planted. He stated all the reasons why it would damage the mother church. Thank God no one listened to his outcry. Prodigals are home now because of the vision of a church that decided it's not about us.

Maybe you are a church member. Maybe you are in the seminary or a longtime pastor. Maybe you are an administrator. Please pray about this. Please act on this. Attend a SEEDS conference, or write the North American Division Evangelism Institute (NADEI) about hosting one.[3]

Prodigals need places to come back to.

RESPONSE

Kymone Hinds, lead pastor and church planter of Journey Fellowship, an Adventist church in Memphis, Tennessee

What do you think?

Everyone needs a place to call home. As Roger describes in this chapter, church planting is creating places for those that "God misses the most" to come home to. It is planning the party and fattening the calf for the return of the son who had left.

There are objections to church planting that I have heard in my own Journey (shameless plug for the plant I am involved with). Many of them are articulated in this chapter. At the core of them is a misunderstanding as to what the goal of the church is all about. There are local churches that believe they exist to grow themselves. That seems reasonable—a church is supposed to grow. But that actually may be a by-product of the main goal.

The goal of the local church is to advance the kingdom of God, which is the rule and reign of God in humanity and in our world. Therefore, each local church needs to work on expansion and multiplication rather than simply preservation and addition. Church planting is one of the primary methods local churches and members can be involved in growing the kingdom of God.

What's so exciting about Triad Adventist Church is that it's lay led. It does not require a salary for a minister. And the worship style is simple. Both of these things make it reproducible. We need models such as these in order to multiply more plants.

Some of the barriers to an exponential growth of new churches are the finances needed to hire new pastors and the complicated methods we use. They give off the unintended message, "Don't try this at home." What we see in the Bible through the work of Paul on his church-planting journeys is that the planted churches were formed in simple ways and led by, in some cases, new converts to Christianity.

I think there is a group of Christians, young and old, that longs to be involved in this extreme sport of ministry. At one conference I attended, Peter Roennfeldt, a church planter, said, "We need to stop trying to keep our youth but release them to start new expressions of church." He may be on to something. Instead of churches holding on to who they have, what if they released them to go plan the party and fatten the calf for the return of the prodigals?

Because everyone needs a place to call home.

What do you do?

I have the blessed privilege of leading a new church plant in Memphis called Journey Fellowship (www.comejourney.org). As our name suggests, we are inviting people on an adventure where we *belong, grow,* and *serve . . . together.* We are engaged in creating opportunities to share the love of God where people live, work, and play.

We are two years in, and it has not been easy. I think anyone engaging in church planting needs to read the list of why not to do a church plant. It is not glamorous and will test your spiritual mettle. So make sure you count the cost before you jump in.

With that said, it has been the most rewarding spiritual experience that I have ever had. It has been a way to see God work in ways I had never imagined. We have learned many lessons (many under the heading of What Not to Do), and we are still learning.

One question I got asked a lot was, What is this church plant all about? I asked God to give me a succinct, simple answer, and He gave me three words: *eat, pray, love* (no relation to the book made into the movie starring Julia Roberts). This is what we do:

Eat—share life together. We are seeking to create a family atmosphere with our church. This is not about an event that happens once a week or a building that we all come to. We are seeking to build relationships of trust. We have discovered that one thing that helps with this is food.

Think about it. If you want to get to know someone, you invite them over for dinner or out for dinner. Sharing food is more than just about eating. It is about growing closer to one another. Even Jesus used table fellowship as a way to show acceptance and offer belonging.

We started off meeting in homes with a meal each time we met. The small core group of individuals grew in our connections with one another. Whether you brought a dish or not, you were welcome.

We have since moved our meals and meeting to a community center. But at our worship gatherings, we have food, and we sit at round tables. We want people to get to know one another at these gatherings. So we eat and share life together.

Pray—seek God together. I believe that God gives incredible answers to prayer, especially in the context of mission. Miracles happen when we are pursuing the plan of God to reach those He misses the most. While on this journey, at one point we hit a wall. It seemed as though we had stagnated. By the way, many church plants go through that. At that time, a friend recommended the book *The Circle Maker,* by Mark Batterson (a must-read for every Christian).

One idea we lifted from the book was praying circles around things that we were asking God for . . . literally. Our group held a prayer planning meeting. We would briefly present the item on the agenda and then go into prayer on it. That was the best planning meeting I've ever been in. Coming out of that meeting, we were looking for a place to meet.

The Lord led my family and I to a community center. We went there on several different days and walked around it and laid hands on it. When we finally approached the directors of the center, they welcomed us with open arms, not as renters but as partners with some of the plans they had been wanting to do. So we pray and seek God together.

Love—serve others together. The question of what many are looking for in a church is, What is it doing for others? I believe every church, especially a church plant, needs to figure out how it will serve others in the community. We have centered our service around the community center that we are partnering with.

We have held family events at the center to bring people together. Just like taking food to hungry people, we see our role as offering community to disconnected people. It has been great to see neighbors meeting each other.

Another service we are doing is our donation drives. At each of our worship services, we collect an item to give to an agency. So far we have collected shoes and canned goods. So we love and serve others together.

Church planting is a journey: following God to reach others for Him.

Questions

1. If church planting is statistically proven to be so effective, why don't we do it more?

2. Even if you are not planting a church, what can you do to support church planters in your city, conference, or around the world?

3. Truthfully speaking, if prodigals returned to your local church, how would they be received? Why do you think that is?

4. Why is having healthy motives so important in church planting?

5. Is God calling you to plant a church in your city?

---

1. Jesse Solomon, "Burger King's CEO Is Only 34," CNNMoney, August 26, 2014, accessed November 24, 2015, http://money.cnn.com/2014/08/25/investing/burger-king-ceo-age-33/.

2. David T. Olson, "Dave Olson's Top Ten Reasons to Plant Churches," adapted from David T. Olson, *The American Church in Crisis* (Grand Rapids, MI: Zondervan, 2008), http://www2.crcna.org/site_uploads/uploads/crhm/guidelines/B1-07.pdf.

3. SEEDS conference information can be found at the NADEI Web site: http://nadei.org/article/396/evangelism-services/church-planting/seeds-church-planting-conference.

Endgame

Someone has said that change is like leading a ship in shark-infested waters, in the middle of a storm, with a leaky boat, a mutinous crew, and the enemy shooting at you.

Every time a person stands up for God and is willing to take a risk in order to improve the present situation and make the necessary changes, that person will encounter opposition. If it is true that at times we have made the church something it is not, we can reverse the trend and begin to take the steps to change the church back to what God intended it to be.

I would like to finish the book diving deep into the story of David and Goliath. I believe in this story we can find powerful principles to deal with the people and situations in our lives that pretend to stop God's work from going forward as fast as it can. Some of those people are well intentioned, but mistaken. Some can be family members. Some are just acquaintances that share membership in the same organization but little else.

David had been anointed as the next king, but Saul, the present king, who was a tall fellow with a small heart, was in the midst of a confrontation with their constant enemies, the Philistines. We know how the story ends, with a great victory of God's people over a mighty enemy that included a giant named Goliath. Before that victory took place, David had to overcome four obstacles, in the form of people, that could have derailed his plans. I suggest to you that if your church wants to become a prevailing, overcoming, power-filled church, you need to be aware of these people.

Some would like to limit you

"Now Jesse said to his son David, 'Take this ephah of roasted grain and these ten loaves of bread for your brothers and hurry to their camp. Take along these ten cheeses to the commander of their unit. See how your brothers are and bring back some assurance from them' " (1 Samuel 17:17, 18, NIV).

The people of Israel were in need of soldiers, not delivery boys. They were in the midst of war. Did you notice what David's father was saying to him? "The only thing you are good for right now is to take supplies and bring back news." Even though David had been anointed king, his father still considered him an errand boy.

Whenever God calls someone in order to use that person, although His vision may be very clear to you, it may not be as clear to those around you! In fact, the ones closer to you might be the ones hardest to convince that you should be doing something different than what you are doing now.

The tragic part in the story of David was that the person who tried to limit him was his own father. A word to parents everywhere. Make sure your children know that you are willing to support them. Help them to dream, teach them to stretch themselves. Remember, where one parent saw an errand boy, God saw a king.

Good thing David had the good sense to "disobey" his dad. The Bible tells us that he went to the front lines and, instead of limiting himself to making deliveries, he got close to the action. He spoke to people; he observed and analyzed the situation. Then he acted.

Some would like to give you advice (that they are not following)

Early in the morning David left the flock in the care of a shepherd, loaded up and set out, as Jesse had directed. He reached the camp as the army was going out to its battle positions, *shouting the war cry.* Israel and the Philistines were drawing up their lines facing each other. David left his things with the keeper of supplies, ran to the battle lines and asked his brothers how they were. As he was talking with them, Goliath, the Philistine champion from Gath, stepped out from his lines and shouted his usual defiance, and David heard it. Whenever the Israelites saw the man, they all fled from him in great fear (1 Samuel 17:20–24, NIV; emphasis added).

Did you notice what the people of Israel did every day? The text says that they "shouted the war cry." Can you imagine that scene? They would get up in the morning, adjust their helmets, put on their boots, sharpen their swords, strap on their chest protectors, and line up for battle. Probably a leader of some kind would come around, and the shouting would start. *Who will win the battle? We will! Who fights for Jehovah? We do. Who shall plunder the enemy? We shall!* The only problem is that everybody was shouting but no one was fighting. When Goliath came out, their words became as your wallet on the Thursday before payday.

You will find some people like that in your church—they have an idea for everything and have implemented *not a one*! God values our words only when they are accompanied with actions. I once had a church member who was very angry and let me know the reason why. He was upset that in his church many people were getting baptized, yet some were leaving because no one was giving them the proper follow-up. After ranting for what seemed like an eternity, I asked him whether he himself had taken *any* of those many under his wing. He mumbled something and left. It is easier to speak about the problems than it is to do something about them.

As I have mentioned before, I love sports. I love to play them, watch them, and coach them. Once in a while I get together with some friends to watch a football game of the best team in the universe, i.e., the Dallas Cowboys. One of the memorable scenes that will happen in every game is when one of my friends, usually the somewhat uncoordinated, slightly overweight, "was cut by the third-grade team while in the eighth grade" guy, gets up and screams at the quarterback/coach/defense to do something. He is very confused and/or angry about why the quarterback did not throw the ball to the open receiver or why the defensive back failed to make a tackle. I wonder how long my friend would last in the NFL. Probably between not a minute and less than no time at all. It is one thing to sit comfortably in the lounge chair and spew commands. It is another to make an accurate pass to the right receiver forty yards downfield with a 350-pound beast gunning for your head.

It is not the critic who counts; not the man who points out the how the strong man stumbles, or where the doer of deeds could have done better. The credit belongs to the man who is actually in the arena, whose face is marred by dust and sweat and blood; who strives valiantly; who errs, and comes short again and again, . . . but who does

actually strive to do the deeds; who knows the great en-
thusiasms, the great devotions; who spends himself in a
worthy cause; who at the best knows in the end the tri-
umph of high achievement; and who at worst, if he fails,
at least fails while daring greatly, so that his place shall
never be with those cold and timid souls who neither
know victory nor defeat.[1]

Some will judge your motives

When Eliab, David's oldest brother, heard him speaking
with the men, he burned with anger at him and asked,
"Why have you come down here? And with whom did
you leave those few sheep in the wilderness? *I know how
conceited you are* and how wicked your heart is; you came
down only to watch the battle."

"Now what have I done?" said David. "Can't I even
speak?" He then turned away to someone else and
brought up the same matter, and the men answered him
as before (1 Samuel 17:28–30, NIV; emphasis added).

If it wasn't one family member, it was another. It makes
you wonder about David's family. All David wants is to get
some information about what is going on, and he can't catch
a break. His oldest brother, the same one who was passed over
when Samuel went to their house, is angry at him and making
a scene. What does Eliab know about David? How can he
know about his intentions? How can anyone *know* what is in
the heart of another person? It's impossible. Yet we do it all
the time. We label people. We assign categories based on race,
money, education, family of origin, or church they belong to.

A pastor by the name of Clarence Schilt says that "we sin the most when we are right." That has stuck with me. It is far easier to box people in, to make them fit in these tight little categories. That way, you don't even have to try to relate to them, because in your mind you already know.

Eliab belongs to the type of people I like to call "drainers." Some people are natural encouragers, so that when you finish a conversation with them you feel uplifted, ready to take on the world. Others, however, have the gift of draining every last ounce of happiness out of your life. Such was Eliab. He could not leave well enough alone. He had to make a comment. He had to make a scene. He had to make sure everyone, including David, knew that David was a nobody, just a shepherd—when he should be affirming the future king. He was judging his own heart.

I love David's response to Eliab. First he said, "What have I done now?" which shows that they have had this type of encounter before. Then he did what most of us should have done to *that* family member or friend who constantly tried to put us down. The Bible says that David "turned away to someone else." People like Eliab you can't please, no matter how hard you try. Walk away.

Some will try to demand you do it their way

"Then Saul dressed David in his *own* tunic. He put a coat of armor on him and a bronze helmet on his head. David fastened on his sword over the tunic and tried walking around, because he was not used to them. 'I cannot go in these,' he said to Saul, 'because I am not used to them.' So he took them off" (1 Samuel 17:38, 39, NIV; emphasis added).

Saul was well-intentioned. He was comfortable in a soldier's uniform, and he assumed David would be too. But he was wrong. David and Saul were both warriors, but they were very different. Whereas Saul liked the sword, David felt comfortable with the sling. Instead of a spear, a smooth stone; instead of a helmet, a bag of rocks. Saul didn't make the mistake of stopping David. He just thought David should do it the way he (Saul) had always done it.

We see this same attitude in people every day. We see it in families. Husbands try to change their wives, sometimes by force. Wives look at their husbands as their projects. Parents try to live vicariously through their children. We see it in the workplace. The old guard unable to accept new methods tries to convince and convert the younger workers to "the right way." We see it, sadly, in churches. Some people try to impose their taste as gospel.

Now, I want to make something completely clear. There are some unchangeable, unbreakable, untouchable principles in God's Word that can't be modified according to the year you are living in or the mood of the populace. Those are fewer in number. There are also some things that are just a matter of preference, such as the time to start Sabbath School, whether we should sing two or four stanzas, and so forth. Do we play the organ or the keyboard? Does the congregation have to kneel for every prayer? What version of the Bible should be used? Those are just some of the millions of details on which good Christians may disagree without being disagreeable.

The problem comes when we try to make people into our image. As an example, look at the different styles of preaching. I use some humor in my presentations because that is who I am. I take my job very seriously, but I have found out by personal experience that humor in the pulpit, when it is done in a tasteful way, breaks down barriers. Invariably, in every church where I have ever been a pastor, that particular style is not appreciated by a few. There is nothing wrong with that, but the problem comes when they write notes and have conversations with me about how I should change how God has made me. God has confirmed my ministry many times, and I am most fulfilled by not being a second anyone but by being the first me.

To David's credit, he did what many of us probably would not have done, especially at that age. He told the king no. I believe the words he used were "I cannot go in these." God's hand was in all of this, because David's response did not make the king go crazy (and we know how bipolar Saul could be). My humble suggestion to you is this: Be yourself. Develop your own gifts. Try to be the best you that you can be. Let's go kill some giants.

---

1. Theodore Roosevelt, "Citizenship in a Republic," speech delivered at the Sorbonne, Paris, France, April 23, 1910.

PREACH

A template for a weeklong reaping series

I would say my preaching has become more Christ centered, more biblically basic, and certainly ministering more to the felt needs of people. —Mark Finley

We all have problems. That's a fact of life. What we do and how we deal with major life challenges will determine the level of growth we will experience. Thankfully, there is help. "We All Have HOPE" is a one-week, practical Bible presentation of some of the most common problems people have and how God's grace affects them in a positive way. You are not alone. Join us. We will get through this together.

Vision

1. Present Bible truth in a way that makes sense and helps believers think and thinkers believe.

2. Train members so they see service and evangelism as a way of life, not an event.

PPP Plan

PREPARATION • PROCLAMATION • PRESERVATION

Nine months before—Plan (preparation)
- Meet with your church leaders to present the plan.
- Rally for launching the PPP plan to the church.
- Provide all of the members a calendar with all of the important dates that will make up the PPP plan.
- Lock in a location.

Eight months before—Train (preparation)
- Monthly training begins preparing the members to all get involved in reaching those God misses the most. (See the topics below.) You can use guest speakers as long as you ask them not just to speak on a specific topic but also to have the members apply it in practical ways using a hands-on method.
- In order to make the most of the training, pastors incorporate what has been taught into the life of the church and begin putting it into practice as the evangelistic series approaches. Sample topics are:

Topic	Category
• Intercessory Prayer	• Preparation
• Preparing for the Harvest	• Preparation
• Community Bible Studies	• Preparation/ Preservation

- Helping People Cross the Line

- Service Evangelism

- Innovative Evangelism

- How to Keep Our Members

- Proclamation

- Preparation/ Preservation

- Proclamation/ Preservation

- Preservation

Six months before—Small Groups (preparation/proclamation)

- Members begin building relationships with the people in our communities through community Bible studies.
- Churches choose the small-group curriculum that works best for their church and small groups.
- Encourage your churches to begin a children and youth baptismal class in preparation for the meetings.

Four months before—Season of Service (preparation/proclamation)

- Season of Service (SOS) is a forty-day service initiative that seeks to demonstrate God's love in practical ways to the city. It can be described in three words: *intentional, impact, involve.*
- The plan has three simple steps:

  1. A *daily* service activity that any one person can do. This is encouraged in the daily devotional called

Season of Service. (You can find information here: IMPRRH@gmail.com.)

2. A service-intensive *weekend* activity with multiple opportunities to serve as churches, groups, families, and individuals. This usually happens about day twenty of the forty days.

   - We provide the brochures with all of the SOS weekend opportunities, along with a Web site where they can sign up to volunteer: www .mycitysos.com.
   - We also provide T-shirts for all those who volunteer.
   - The first round of advertisement for the evangelistic series begins during this weekend.

3. A *Sabbath* celebration of service in local churches or all together, where the members affirm and thank volunteers for their service at the end of the forty days. Civic leaders and leaders of local service organizations are invited to attend and be prayed for at that time.

   - By this time, have the handbills ready for everyone to begin handing out.

Three months before—Bible Workers Arrive (preparation)

Bible workers can be a blessing to your meeting. You can train one or contact the SALT (Soul-winning And Leadership Training) program at Southern Adventist University.

Everyone Welcome

Forty days before—God's City, My City—Prayer and Sharing Campaign and Small Groups (preparation/proclamation)

God's City, My City (GCMC) has three components:

1. *Six small-group lessons* found in the first part of the book called *My City, God's City* (see the lessons in *Season of Service*). One lesson for each week that will lead up to the week of the evangelistic series. These lessons encourage the members of the small group to

   Love the city   Pray for the city   Engage the city

   Serve the city   Invite the city   Transform the city

   - **Free:** For the small-group leader or pastor, a short version of how to teach each lesson. Watch it here: https://www.youtube.com/user/pastorRoger Hernandez/videos.
   - **Free:** Small-group leader training manual. A simple how-to for the small-group leader. Download it here for free: http://www.slideshare.net/Roger Hernandez6/my-citygods-cityhowto.

2. *Forty-day prayer and sharing devotional* that is found in the back of the book *Season of Service*. We encourage everyone to be praying for each aspect of the evangelistic series and to share their faith daily. The devotional provides

   - A memory verse to ground him or her in God's Word;

164

- Applications to teach him or her God's Word;
- A practical assignment to put God's Word into action in his or her life;
- A prayer phone line on which people call in, and we do these daily devotionals and pray together as a city.

3. *Sermon series* with the same six titles as the small-group lessons, to be developed by the pastor and preached concurrently with the small-group series.

Forty days before—Advertising and Preregistration (preparation)

- Blanket neighborhoods with handbills and posters, radio and newspaper ads, etc.
- At this time begin to preregister *everyone,* including members. Why everyone?

  - So guests won't feel as though they are being singled out.
  - So that a spirit of fellowship can be created in which everyone knows your name.
  - To keep a better record of attendance.
  - To gain a greater sense of commitment among those who are preregistered.

Two to three weeks before—Volunteer Training Day (preparation)

- Committees are formed and directors are assigned.

- Each committee director will get the opportunity to meet with their volunteers and go over details and their responsibilities during the week of the series.
- The training is an important factor to the organization and excellence of each area of the series.

Sample of Nightly Program

Church Responsible:	[church name]	
Time	**Activity**	**Person Responsible**
6:40 P.M.	Movie	A/V team
7:00 P.M.	Song service (one song and theme song)	
7:10 P.M.	Welcome and prayer/dismiss children	
7:15 P.M.	Health segment	
7:22 P.M.	Prayer/offering (instrumental music)	
7:25 P.M.	Special music	Guest singer
7:30 P.M.	Message	
8:15 P.M.	Special music/altar call Baptism (music/song) Big gift	
8:30 P.M.	Farewell (music)	

Presentations

Date	Sermon	Description	Adventist Connection
Saturday P.M.	We All Have Issues . . .	Let's be real for a moment. We all have problems. We will study three of the most common problems you and I have and how God's grace impacts them in a positive way. An invitation to be REAL.	Grace
Sunday	Epic Fail	Failure can be your teacher, but it doesn't have to define you. Understand the reasons, opportunities, and reactions to failure. God can help you, here and now. An invitation to VICTORY.	Great controversy
Monday	Rest	Rather than being just another rat in the rat race, discover the secret to balance. God wants you to Stop. Worship. Rest. An invitation to BALANCE.	Sabbath
Tuesday	Dollars and Sense	Someone said we spend money we don't have on things we don't need to impress people we don't even like. Come and understand our part, the perils, and the purpose of money. An invitation to PROSPER.	Finances

Wednesday	Building Bridges	Because sometimes you and your kin can't. Come and learn three characteristics of a successful family. There will be something for everyone—couples, children, and singles. An invitation to BELONG.	Family
Thursday	My Body, God's House	God cares about what's in your body, on your body, and what others do to your body. An invitation to HEALTH.	Health, healing, heaven
Friday	Beyond the Grave	So far, the ratio of people being born and dying is one to one. We try to avoid thinking and talking about it, but it's coming. Come and learn what happens after you die and why it's important. An invitation to LIVE.	State of the dead
Saturday P.M.	Hope Wins!	Hope is not a political slogan or a pipe dream. Hope is what sustains, inspires, and propels. God doesn't consult your past to build your future. An invitation to DECIDE.	Baptism

Since the people will have studied the doctrines in the home in the last six months, the sermons are decision sermons while addressing the main beliefs. If you want a copy of the messages, e-mail me and I will be glad to send them.

Appendix

Community Survey 1

You have the privilege of participating in a research study that aims to assess the level of satisfaction with present community and home conditions and the degree of spiritual interest in the community in order to generate comprehensive programs that meet the needs of the people. We would greatly appreciate your participation in completing the following questionnaire.

Name _____

Address _____

City _____ State _____ Zip Code _____

E-mail _____

Phone _____

1. What are, in your estimation, the greatest needs and problems in this community?

   _____

2. If you could change one thing in your life, what would it be?

   _____

3. What is the greatest source of stress for you these days?

   _____

4. In what areas would you like to improve your health?

Everyone Welcome

❏ Exercise ❏ Nutrition ❏ Sleep ❏ Beverages ❏ Smoking
❏ Stress management ❏ Other _____

5. Which of the following programs or activities would you
   be interested in attending if they were held in this area?

   ❏ Healthful cooking class   ❏ Weight-loss program
   ❏ Stress management class   ❏ Stop smoking clinic
   ❏ Money management seminar   ❏ Depression recovery seminar
   ❏ Personal Bible studies   ❏ Bible prophecy seminar
   ❏ Vacation Bible School   ❏ Social activities

6. Would you like to talk to someone about any other needs
   you may have?   ❏ Yes   ❏ No

Community Survey 2

You have the privilege of participating in a research study that aims to assess the level of satisfaction with present community and home conditions and the degree of spiritual interest in the community in order to generate comprehensive programs that meet the needs of the people. We would greatly appreciate your participation in completing the following questionnaire.

Name _____
Address _____
City _____ State _____ Zip Code _____
E-mail _____
Phone _____

1. What are, in your estimation, the greatest needs and problems in this community?

   _____

2. If you could change one thing in your life, what would it be?

   _____

3. What is the greatest source of stress for you these days?

   _____

4. In what areas would you like to improve your health?

   ❑ Exercise ❑ Nutrition ❑ Sleep ❑ Beverages ❑ Smoking
   ❑ Stress management ❑ Other _____

5. Would you like a free Bible study course that you can study in the privacy of your own home that is designed for busy people?

   ❏ Yes   ❏ Not now

6. Which of the following programs or activities would you be interested in attending if they were held in this area?

   ❏ Healthful cooking class   ❏ Weight-loss program
   ❏ Stress management class   ❏ Stop smoking clinic
   ❏ Money management seminar   ❏ Depression recovery seminar
   ❏ Personal Bible studies   ❏ Bible prophecy seminar
   ❏ Vacation Bible School   ❏ Social activities

7. Would you like us to pray with and for you? What requests do you have? _____

   _____

8. Would you like to talk to someone about any other needs you may have?   ❏ Yes   ❏ No

Community Survey 3

1. What are, in your estimation, the greatest needs/problems in this community?

   _____   _____

   _____   _____

2. What is the greatest source of stress for you these days?

   _____

3. In what areas would you like to improve your health?

   ❑ Exercise ❑ Nutrition ❑ Sleep ❑ Beverages ❑ Smoking
   ❑ Stress management ❑ Other _____

4. In light of current world events, would you say that Bible prophecy is being fulfilled?   ❑ Yes   ❑ Not now

5. Which of these sound interesting to you?

   ❑ Healthful cooking class   ❑ Weight-loss program
   ❑ Stress management class   ❑ Stop smoking clinic
   ❑ Money management seminar   ❑ Depression recovery seminar
   ❑ Personal Bible studies   ❑ Bible prophecy seminar
   ❑ Vacation Bible School   ❑ Social activities
   ❑ Pathfinders   ❑ Christian school
   ❑ Mommy and Me

6. What would you like prayer for?

   _____

   _____

7. If you are interested, when would be a good time to study
   the Bible with you?

   _____

Name _____
Address _____
City _____ State ____ Zip Code _____
E-mail _____
Phone _____

Community Survey 4

1. What are, in your estimation, the greatest needs and problems in this community?

    _____   _____

    _____   _____

2. What is the greatest source of stress for you these days?

    _____

3. In what areas would you like to improve your health?

    ❑ Exercise ❑ Nutrition ❑ Sleep ❑ Beverages ❑ Smoking
    ❑ Stress management ❑ Other _____

4. Which of these sound interesting?

    ❑ Healthful cooking class   ❑ Weight-loss program
    ❑ Stress management class   ❑ Stop smoking clinic
    ❑ Money management seminar   ❑ Depression recovery seminar
    ❑ Personal Bible studies   ❑ Vacation Bible School
    ❑ Social activities   ❑ Pathfinders
    ❑ Christian school   ❑ Mommy and Me

Name _____
Address _____
City _____ State ____ Zip Code _____
E-mail _____
Phone _____